FAST-FORWARD TO THE FUTURE

D1378999

KAY ARTHUR
JANNA ARNDT

HARVEST HOUSE PUBLISHERS

EUGENE, OREGON

Scripture quotations in this book are taken from the New American Standard Bible ®, © 1960, 1962, 1963, 1968, 1971, 1972, 1973, 1975, 1977, 1995 by The Lockman Foundation. Used by permission. (www.Lockman.org)

DISCOVER 4 YOURSELF is a registered trademark of The Hawkins Children's LLC. Harvest House Publishers, Inc., is the exclusive licensee of the federally registered trademark DISCOVER 4 YOURSELF.

Illustrations © 2007 by Steve Bjorkman

Cover by Left Coast Design, Portland, Oregon

FAST-FORWARD TO THE FUTURE

Copyright © 2008 by Precept Ministries International
Published by Harvest House Publishers
Eugene, Oregon 97402
www.harvesthousepublishers.com

ISBN-13: 978-0-7369-2285-2
ISBN-10: 0-7369-2285-7

Printed in the United States of America

08   09   10   11   12   13   14   15   16   / ML-NI /   10   9   8   7   6   5   4   3   2   1

In loving memory of
Ryan Lamar,
an awesome young man with a heart for God.
It was a joy and a pleasure to teach you!
You blessed me with your smiles, your hugs, and your stories.

I love you, buddy,

Mrs. Arndt ☺

"His master said to him, 'Well done, good and faithful slave.
You were faithful with a few things, I will put you in charge
of many things; enter into the joy of your master.'"
Matthew 25:23

CONTENTS

Studying God's Script—
A Bible Study *You* Can Do!

STUDYING GOD'S SCRIPT—
A BIBLE STUDY YOU CAN DO!

Hey, guys, welcome back to the set! Molly and I are so excited to have you back in Hollywood, California, to continue our awesome Bible adventure on the Book of Daniel. By the way, my name is Max, and this is Sam, the great face-licking detective beagle.

We had so much fun as we filmed *You're a Brave Man, Daniel!* and discovered that Daniel is an exciting historical book in the Bible that shows us not only WHAT happened in the past but also WHAT is going to happen in the future.

As we begin filming the second season of our television series, we are going to find out WHO has visions and dreams in Daniel 7–12. WHAT do these dreams mean? WHO are the four beasts that come up out of the sea? WHAT do they represent? WHO are the other two kingdoms represented on the statue in Daniel 2? And WHO is the little horn with eyes like a man and a mouth of boastful words?

This is going to be an *amazing* television series with some unbelievable special effects as we film some very mysterious dreams! You can take part in creating this fantastic series by studying God's Word, the Bible, the source of all truth, and by asking God's Spirit to lead and guide you. You also have this book, which is an inductive Bible study. That word *inductive* means you go straight to the Bible *yourself* to investigate what the Book of Daniel shows us about God and His plan for the future. In inductive Bible study you discover for yourself what the Bible says and means.

Aren't you excited? Grab your script on Daniel and get ready for a very cool adventure as we uncover some mysterious visions that show us what is going to happen in the future!

THINGS YOU'LL NEED

New American Standard Bible (Updated Edition)—
preferably the New Inductive Study Bible (NISB)
Have you gotten yours yet?

Pen or Pencil   A Dictionary

Colored Pencils   This Workbook

Index Cards

1

FOUR FEROCIOUS BEASTS

Daniel 2 & 7

"Whoa! Look out!" Max warned. "Here comes Sam! He missed you so much! He's about to jump up and give your face a good licking! Okay, Sam—get down, boy! Come on, give them a break. They know you missed them." Sam quit jumping as he turned in circles and wagged his tail. "Now that Sam has officially welcomed you back to the set, let's go see what Aunt Sherry and Miss Leslie are up to. We can't wait to find out what will happen next!"

DAY ONE

SCAN THE SCRIPT!

"Hey, guys!" Aunt Sherry smiled as she and Miss Leslie walked back on the set. "Are you ready to start working on Season Two on the Book of Daniel?"

"We sure are!" Max replied as he put Sam back on his leash.

"Great! Then grab your scripts. Now WHAT is the first thing you need to do before you open your script?"

"Pray," Molly answered.

"Right! Remember, Bible study should always begin with prayer. We need to ask God to help us understand what the Bible says and to direct us by His Holy Spirit, so we can make sure we understand His Word and handle it accurately."

"Okay, guys," Aunt Sherry said after praying, "do you remember that Daniel is both a historical and prophetic book? In our first season we focused on the historical events. As we begin filming our new season for Daniel 7–12, we are going to focus on prophecy. We are going to see more visions and dreams as God fast-forwards us into the future and shows us things that haven't happened yet.

"But before we can get started on our new episode, we need to review. Do you remember what two languages the Book of Daniel was written in?"

Max smiled. "That's easy. Daniel is a book in the Old Testament, so it was written in Hebrew with some Aramaic."

"Awesome!" Miss Leslie exclaimed. "Now, looking at Daniel 1–7, do you remember which chapters of Daniel were written in Hebrew and which ones were in Aramaic?"

"I remember," Molly answered. "Daniel 1 is written in Hebrew, and Daniel 2–7 is written in Aramaic."

"Amazing," Miss Leslie replied.

"I told you they were good." Aunt Sherry winked at Max and

Molly. "Why was Daniel 1 written in the Hebrew language and Daniel 2–7 in Aramaic?"

"Daniel 1 is written in Hebrew because it is about the sons of Israel, and Hebrew is the language of the Jewish people."

"You got it," Aunt Sherry replied. "Now it's your turn, Max."

"King Nebuchadnezzar captures the city of Jerusalem and takes Daniel and the sons of Israel into captivity to Babylon, where they are taught the language of the Chaldeans. Daniel 2–7 focuses on the Gentile nations, so it is written in Aramaic, which is the language of Nebuchadnezzar and the Gentile nations."

"All right! You guys are awesome!" Miss Leslie exclaimed. "Let's review WHAT happens in Daniel 2 after Daniel and his friends enter into the king's personal service."

To remind ourselves of this awesome dream, we need to read Daniel 2 in our Observation Worksheets and ask the 5 W's and an H. WHAT are the 5 W's and an H? They are the WHO, WHAT, WHERE, WHEN, WHY, and HOW questions.

1. Remember, Daniel is both a historical and prophetic book, so asking WHO is very important. Asking WHO helps you find out:

   WHO are the main characters?

   WHO is this prophecy about?

   WHO is involved?

2. WHAT helps you understand:

   WHAT are the main events taking place?

   WHAT is God telling you?

3. WHEN tells us about time. We mark it with a green clock 🕐 or a green circle like this: ◯. WHEN tells us:

   WHEN did this event happen or WHEN is it going to happen?

   WHEN is so very important in history and prophecy. It helps us follow the order of events.

4. In any historical event, WHERE is very important. And in prophecy it is also important to know WHERE it happens. WHERE helps you learn:

WHERE did something happen?

WHERE did they go?

WHERE was this said?

When we discover a WHERE, we double-underline the WHERE in green.

5. Looking at history, WHY asks questions like:

WHY did this event happen?

Looking at prophecy, WHY asks:

WHY is God telling us this is going to happen?

6. HOW lets you figure out things like:

HOW did something happen?

HOW did the people react to what happens?

HOW is something going to happen in the future?

HOW does it come to pass?

Turn to page 168. Read Daniel 2 and ask those 5 W's and an H.

Daniel 2:1 WHO has a dream? _____

Daniel 2:2 WHOM did the king call in to tell him his dream?_____

_____

Could they tell King Nebuchadnezzar his dream and its meaning? _____

Daniel 2:24-26 WHO told King Nebuchadnezzar his dream and the interpretation? _____

Daniel 2:28 WHO revealed the mystery of the dream to Daniel?

_____

Daniel 2:29 WHAT would this dream show King Nebuchadnezzar?

What will take place? _____

Daniel 2:31 WHAT was the dream about?

A great _____

Isn't it amazing that God is going to show King Nebuchadnezzar what is going to happen in the future? Tomorrow we are going to wrap up our review by looking at this awesome statue to help us remember what we learned in *You're a Brave Man, Daniel!* and so we can see how this statue fits in with the vision we will discover in Daniel 7. Hang in there! There is so much more to come!

But before we leave the set today, we need to solve this week's memory verse. Look at the crown maze on the next page that represents God's kingdom. Find the correct path in the crown to see WHO will receive the kingdom and for HOW long, according to Daniel 7. Then fill in the blanks with the correct words from your maze and find the reference for this verse. Practice saying this verse out loud three times in a row, three times every day this week!

_____

_____ _____ _____ _____

_____ _____ _____ _____

_____ _____ _____, _____ _____

_____ _____ _____.

Daniel 7:_____

Way to go! We are so proud of you!

ON THE SET

It's great to have you back! Are you ready to take another look at the awesome statue in Daniel 2? Do you remember that this statue shows us four kingdoms that will rule on earth before Jesus returns to set up His kingdom? Last season in *You're a Brave Man, Daniel!* we discovered WHO two of those kingdoms are on the statue, as well as what part of the statue represented God's kingdom. Today we want to review what we learned about the statue in Daniel 2.

> Don't forget to talk to God and ask for His help. Then turn to page 171. Read Daniel 2:31-45.
>
> Daniel 2:32 WHAT was the head made of? _____
>
> Daniel 2:38 WHAT part of the statue represented King Nebuchadnezzar?
>
> "You are the _____ of _____."
>
> WHERE does King Nebuchadnezzar rule? WHAT is the name of his kingdom? You can look in your Bible at Daniel 1:1 if you don't remember.
>
> _____

Look at the picture of this awesome statue on page 18. Look at the column for Daniel 2 and color the head. Somewhere in the space beside the head write "Gold: Nebuchadnezzar, king of Babylon."

Daniel 2:32 WHAT is the second part of the statue?

Its _____ and its _____ of _____

Daniel 2:39 WHAT will there be after King Nebuchadnezzar?

_____ _____ that is _____
to King Nebuchadnezzar's.

Do you remember WHAT kingdom this is? Pull out your
Bible and fast-forward over to Daniel 5:28. Remember, this hasn't
happened at the time of Nebuchadnezzar's dream. In Daniel 5
we see that this is the time when Belshazzar is king of Babylon.
To WHOM does it say Belshazzar's kingdom is given?

The _____ and the _____

Darius the Mede takes over the kingdom of Babylon in Daniel
5:30-31. The head of gold falls, and now the Medes and Persians
are in control.

Turn to page 18. Color the second part of the statue. Write in
the space next to the breast and arms of silver "Silver: Inferior
kingdom, kingdom of Medes and Persians."

Daniel 2:32 WHAT is the third part of the statue?

Its _____ and its _____ of _____.

Daniel 2:39 WHAT do you learn about the third kingdom?

A kingdom of _____, which will _____
over all the _____.

Turn to page 18. Color the third part of the statue. Write in the
space next to the belly and thighs of bronze "Bronze: Kingdom
will rule over all the earth."

At this time we don't know who this third kingdom is, but we
will someday.

Daniel 2:33 WHAT is the fourth part of the statue?

Its _____ of _____, its _____ partly of
_____ and partly of _____.

Look at Daniel 2:40-43. WHAT do you learn about the fourth kingdom?

It is as _____ as i __ __ n. It will _____ and _____ all these in _____.

Daniel 2:41 It will be a d __ __ __ __ __ d kingdom.

Daniel 2:42 Some of it will be _____ and some of it will be _____.

Turn to page 18. Color this part of the statue. Write in the space on the left side, next to the legs of iron, "Iron: Strong kingdom will crush and shatter." And by the feet of iron and clay write, "Divided kingdom, part strong, part brittle."

Daniel 2:42-44 WHAT do the toes of the feet represent? Read these verses again. Verse 42 is talking about the toes, and in verse 43 it says *they*, referring to the toes, and in verse 44 it says WHAT?

"In the days of those _____."

The toes are k __ __ __ s!

HOW many toes does a person have? _____ toes

So HOW many kings will there be? _____ kings

Daniel 2:44-45 WHAT do we learn about God's kingdom?

It will never be _____; it will not be left for another _____; it will _____ and put an _____ to all these _____, but it will itself endure _____.

Daniel 8

Daniel 7

Daniel 2

Daniel 2:45 WHAT part of our picture represents God's kingdom? WHAT did we learn about the stone? WHAT did it do?

"It c _ _ _ _ _ d the i _ _ n, the b _ _ _ _ e, the c_ _ y, the s _ _ _ _ _ r and the g _ _ d."

Turn to your statue on page 18. Color the stone. In the space beside the stone write "God's kingdom will never be destroyed. Crushes all of the kingdoms. Endures forever!"

Amazing! God has just shown you what is going to happen in the future. So far you have discovered who two of those kingdoms are on the statue: the kingdom of Babylon and the kingdom of the Medes and Persians. You also saw that the stone represents God's kingdom, which will crush and shatter all of the kingdoms. God's kingdom will never be destroyed. It endures forever!

WHO are the third and fourth kingdoms on the statue? Just wait. You'll find out. Don't forget to practice your memory verse.

DAY THREE

SKETCHING THE SCENE

"Okay, guys," Aunt Sherry said as we climbed into our director's chairs, "today we are going to start working on our new episode. We are going to need some awesome special effects as we start filming Daniel 7."

"Oh, man!" Max exclaimed. "This is going to be so much fun. I can't wait. We're going to get a glimpse into the future, Sam." Sam, sensing Max's excitement, started barking and wagging his tail. "What do you want us to do next?"

"I'm meeting with Miss Lenyer to talk about the digital special effects, so why don't you two mark your scripts and draw your storyboards?"

"All right," Molly said. "I'll pray and then we can get started."

Doesn't it sound exciting to know that God is going to show us what is going to happen in the future? Let's get to work. We need to mark our scripts by looking for key words.

What are *key words?* Key words are words that pop up more than once. They are called key words because they help unlock the meaning of the chapter or book that you are studying and give you clues about what is most important in a passage of Scripture.

- Key words are usually used over and over again. (That's because God doesn't want you to miss the point.)

- Key words are important.

- Key words are used by the writer for a reason.

Once you discover a key word, you need to mark it in a special way using a special color or symbol so that you can immediately spot it in Scripture. Don't forget to mark any pronouns that go with the key words, too! WHAT are pronouns? Check out Max and Molly's notes below.

Pronouns

Pronouns are words that take the place of nouns. A noun is a person, place, or thing. A pronoun stands in for a noun! Here's an example: "Molly and Max are so excited about uncovering the mysteries in Daniel 7. They can't wait to discover what the four beasts and ten horns represent." The word *they* is a pronoun because it takes the place of Molly and Max's names in the second sentence. It is another word we use to refer to Molly and Max.

Watch for these other pronouns when you are marking people's names:

I	you	he	she
me	yours	him	her
mine		his	hers
we	it		
our	its		
they	them		

Now look at the key-word box below. These are the key words that you will mark as you work on your script for Daniel 7:1-8. You may also want to make a bookmark for these key words so that you can see them at a glance as you mark them on your Observation Worksheets.

To make a key-word bookmark, get an index card or a piece of paper and write the key words listed in the box below, as well as how you are going to mark them on your Observation Worksheets.

Then turn to your Observation Worksheets on page 172. Observation Worksheets are pages (your script) that have the Bible text printed out for you to use as you mark your key words.

Today you are going to read Daniel 7:1-8 and mark the key words you find in these verses on your Observation Worksheets.

Key Words for Daniel 7:1-8

Daniel (color it blue)

I was looking (I kept looking) (circle it in blue)

dream (vision) (draw a blue cloud around it)

beasts (the rest of the beasts) (color all beasts green, except for the fourth beast—the fourth beast is different)

> fourth beast (color it brown)
>
> different from one another (different from all the beasts)
> (color it pink)
>
> ten horns (color it orange)
>
> another horn (little horn, other horn) (color it red)

Don't forget to mark your pronouns! Mark anything that tells you WHEN by drawing a green clock 🕐 or green circle like this: ◯.

Now ask the 5 W's and an H so we can sketch our scenes.

Daniel 7:1 WHEN is this happening?

In the _____ _____ of _____ king of _____

Daniel 7 begins with the first year of Belshazzar's reign. In Daniel 5 we saw the last night of Belshazzar's reign. Since Daniel 7 is the beginning of Belshazzar's reign, we know that it has to happen historically before Daniel 5. The time in Daniel 7 is around 553 B.C., and Daniel is around 67 years old. It has been about 50 years since Nebuchadnezzar's dream of the statue.

Daniel 7:1 WHAT does Daniel see as he lies on his bed?

_____

In Daniel 1–6 WHO had the dreams? Do you remember? If not, look up Daniel 2:1 and Daniel 4:4-5 in your Bible, and write out WHO had the dreams.

_____

This is the first time that Daniel has the dream instead of being the one to interpret the dream. Wow! And it didn't happen until he was around 67 years old. Pretty amazing, huh?

Daniel 7:2 WHAT did Daniel see as he kept looking in his vision?

_____

Daniel 7:3 WHAT did Daniel see coming out of the sea?

_____

WHAT do we learn about these beasts?

They were _____ from one another.

Wow! Miss Lenyer, the digital artist, wants you to help by drawing storyboards of these four beasts in the boxes below. Storyboards are sketches of the main scenes in our television series.

Draw each beast the way it is described. On the line underneath the box, write out WHAT kind of beast it is. We know these beasts are hard to draw, but just do your best. This will help you really know what each one of these beasts looks like.

Daniel 7:4

Daniel 7:5

Beast #1: _____

Beast #2: _____

Daniel 7:6
Beast #3: _____

Daniel 7:7
Beast #4: dreadful and
t __ __ __ __ __ __ __ __ g

Look at Daniel 7:7. WHAT does the fourth beast do to the remainder (the other three beasts)?

_____

One thing we see about the fourth beast is that it's so different it doesn't even have an animal description.

HOW else was it different than the other beasts?

It had _____ _____.

Daniel 7:8 WHAT does Daniel see as he contemplates (thinks) about the horns?

_____

We start off with _____ horns, then another comes up, so

_____ horns + _____ horn = _____ horns

That gives us HOW many? _____ horns

HOW many are pulled out by the roots? _____ horns

So _____ horns

- _____ horns (the ones pulled out by the roots)

= _____ horns

HOW many horns are left? _____ horns

Look at the horn that comes up after the ten horns in Daniel 7:8.

HOW is this horn described?

Another horn, a _____ one

This horn possessed _____ like the _____ of a _____ and a _____ uttering great _____.

Whoa! Have you ever seen a horn or beasts like the ones we have just seen in Daniel's vision? Pretty amazing, huh? Did you end up with eight horns when you added and subtracted the horns? Way to go!

You have done an awesome job! We'll find out more about these beasts and horns as we keep studying Daniel.

DAY FOUR

SCENE TWO: THE VISION CONTINUES

You did a fantastic job drawing those four ferocious beasts for our storyboards yesterday. Were you scared or surprised by Daniel's vision? This will be a very cool episode!

When we left Daniel yesterday, he was still having his vision.

We need to grab our scripts and find out what else Daniel sees as he keeps on looking. Don't forget to talk to God.

Pull out your key-word bookmark and add any new key words from the box below to your list. Now turn to page 173. Read Daniel 7:9-10 and mark the key words listed below on your Observation Worksheet.

Key Words for Daniel 7:9-10

Ancient of Days (Highest One, Most High) (draw a purple triangle and color it yellow)

I kept looking (circle it in blue)

Don't forget to mark your pronouns! And mark anything that tells you WHEN by drawing a green clock 🕐 or green circle like this: ◯ .

Now help Miss Lenyer by looking at Daniel's night visions.

Daniel 7:9 WHAT did Daniel see set up? _____

WHO took His seat?
The _____ of _____

Describe Him in the blanks below.

His vesture was like _____ _____.
His hair was like _____ _____.

WHAT was His throne like?
His throne was _____ with _____,
its _____ were a _____ _____.

Daniel 7:10 WHAT was flowing out before Him?
A _____ of _____

Daniel 7:10 WHO were attending and standing before Him?

_____ upon _____ were attending

Him and _____ upon _____ were

standing before Him.

Do you know how many a myriad is? (The Greek word literally means 10,000, but it is often used to mean "countless" or "innumerable." That's a big word you can add to your vocabulary. Ask and see if anyone else knows this word.) Can you imagine seeing more than you could possibly count?

Daniel 7:10 WHO sat?

The _____

WHAT was opened?

The _____

You have just seen a very awesome description of the Ancient of Days. Draw a storyboard of this awesome scene of Daniel 7:9-10 in the box below.

WHAT will happen when the books are opened? You'll find out tomorrow. Don't forget to practice your memory verse!

SCENE THREE: THE BOOKS WERE OPENED

"Hey, Molly, look over here!" Max called out as he and Molly walked back on the set.

"Wow! That is awesome. I love the set. I bet that's the throne for the Ancient of Days. Just think how amazing it will look when Aunt Sherry starts filming this scene."

"Yeah, and look at that over there. Doesn't that look like it's going to be the river of fire? Sam will go ballistic when they get the fire flowing."

Molly laughed. "He sure will. Won't you, Sam, old boy?"

Sam started jumping up and wagging his tail when Molly began talking to him. Max scratched behind his ears. "Come on, we'd better get started on our script so we can draw what happens when the books are opened. I'll pray and then we can get to work."

Grab your scripts and let's find out WHAT happens when the books are opened. Pull out your key-word bookmark and add any new key words from the box below to your list. Turn to page 174. Read Daniel 7:11-14 and mark the key words listed below on your Observation Worksheet.

Key Words for Daniel 7:11-14

Son of Man (draw a purple cross and color it yellow)

kingdom (draw a purple crown and color it blue)

I kept looking (circle it in blue)

horn (another horn, little horn) (color it red)

beast (when it is the fourth beast) (color it brown)

beasts (all of the other beasts) (color it green)

visions (draw a blue cloud around it)

Ancient of Days (draw a purple triangle and color it yellow)

Don't forget to mark your pronouns! And mark anything that tells you WHEN by drawing a green clock or green circle like this: ○.

Ask those 5 W's and an H.

Daniel 7:11 WHAT does Daniel see?

_____

WHAT happened to the fourth beast?

It "was _____, and its body was _____

and given to the _____ _____."

Daniel 7:12 WHAT happened to the rest of the beasts?

"Their _____ was taken away, but an extension of _____ was granted to them for an _____ period of _____."

Daniel 7:13 WHOM did Daniel see coming with the clouds of heaven? WHO was presented to the Ancient of Days?

One like a _____ of _____

Daniel 7:14 WHAT was given to Him?

_____, _____ and a _____

WHO is going to serve Him?

All the _____, _____, and men of every language.

HOW long will His dominion last?

It is _____.

WHAT do we see about His kingdom?

It will not be _____.

Now draw these two fantastic events for Miss Lenyer in the boxes below.

Daniel 7:11-12   Daniel 7:13-14

Amazing! WHAT an event! The books are opened, the fourth beast is destroyed, and the rest of the beasts lose their dominion. But we also see a kingdom that will never be destroyed, whose dominion is forever! Wow!

WHOSE kingdom is this? Do you know?

_____

Think about WHAT we learned about the stone in King Nebuchadnezzar's dream of the statue. Do you remember the stone that was cut without hands that struck the statue on the feet and crushed them? Do you remember WHAT that stone represented?

If you aren't sure, look back at the drawing of the statue to what you wrote beside the stone on page 18.

Daniel's interpretation of Nebuchadnezzar's dream showed that each part of the statue represented four different Gentile kingdoms on earth. So far we have discovered two of those kingdoms. The head of gold was the kingdom of B __ __ __ __ __, and the breast and arms of silver was the kingdom of the M __ __ __ __ and P __ __ __ __ __ __ __.

We also saw as we looked at the feet and ten toes that those ten toes were kings, and in the days of those ten kings God would set up a kingdom that would never be destroyed (Daniel 2:44).

Doesn't that sound a lot like Daniel's night vision—a kingdom that will never be destroyed, with an everlasting dominion? Do you think that this kingdom that Daniel dreamed about is the same one the stone represents in Nebuchadnezzar's statue?

_____

Aren't you excited? God is showing you what is going to happen in the future. You have just seen a very awesome description of the Ancient of Days, the judgment that is coming to those very scary beasts, and the kingdom that will be given to the Son of Man.

WHO are those beasts? WHAT do they represent? We'll find out next week as Daniel receives the interpretation for his dream. Hang in there! There are so many more cool and awesome mysteries to uncover as our television series continues.

Don't forget to say your memory verse to a grown-up to remind you that the saints of the Highest One will possess the kingdom forever!

2

THE LITTLE HORN

DANiEL 7

Wow! Last week was amazing as we arrived back on the set and reviewed the statue in King Nebuchadnezzar's dream in Season One of *You're a Brave Man, Daniel!* Were you surprised when you got the pages for our new script and saw Daniel having a dream this time? WHAT did you think about those four very scary beasts that come up out of the sea? How about that awesome vision of the Ancient of Days, and the kingdom that will be given to the Son of Man that will never ever be destroyed?

WHO are those beasts? WHAT do they represent? We'll find out as we begin filming this very exciting episode. Are you ready to get started? Great. Don't forget to ask God for His help. It's time to zoom in on Daniel 7 as Daniel gets the interpretation for his dream.

DAY ONE

ZOOMiNG iN

"All right, quiet on the set. We are ready to roll," Aunt Sherry called out. "Camera One, pick up on Daniel. Come in tight. I want you to zoom in right after the opening sequence. We need a close-up to show how Daniel responds to these visions. Let's count it down, and...action."

Pull out your key-word bookmark and add any new key words to your list. Turn to page 174. Read Daniel 7:15-18 and mark your script so we can zoom in on the action.

Key Words for Daniel 7:15-18

saints (draw a blue star of David)

Daniel (color it blue)

visions (draw a blue cloud around it)

beasts (color it green)

Highest One (draw a purple triangle and color it yellow)

kingdom (draw a purple crown and color it blue)

Don't forget to mark your pronouns! And mark anything that tells you WHEN by drawing a green clock or green circle like this: .

Daniel 7:15 HOW did Daniel react to these visions?

_____

Daniel 7:16 WHOM did Daniel approach?

_____

WHAT did Daniel ask him?

_____

Draw the storyboard for this scene of Daniel 7:15-16 in the box below.

Daniel 7:16-17 WHAT was the interpretation? WHAT is the meaning of the four beasts?

The four beasts are _____ _____ who

will arise from the _____.

Isn't that cool? These four beasts represent four kings, and you know that kings rule over kingdoms. How do these four kingdoms compare to the dream of Nebuchadnezzar's statue that showed us four Gentile kingdoms that would rule on earth? We'll find out tomorrow as we take a closer look at each one of these four beasts.

Daniel 7:18 WHO will receive the kingdom?

_____

HOW long will they possess the kingdom?

_____

All right! Before we wrap it up today, discover this week's memory verse. Look at the roll of film on the next page. Aunt Sherry has found some bad places in the film and cut them out, leaving blank spaces.

You need to splice the film by looking at each one of these pieces of film and writing the word from each piece in the correct space on the roll to complete your verse. To help you solve this verse, we have given you the first letter of each word.

Once you've spliced the film, turn to page 175 in your script and find the reference that goes with this verse.

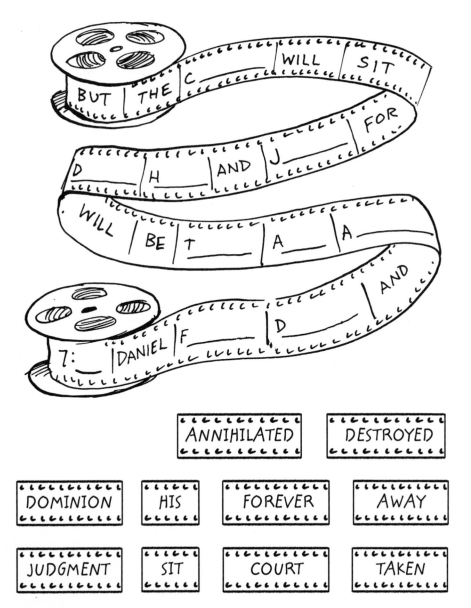

ANNIHILATED   DESTROYED

DOMINION   HIS   FOREVER   AWAY

JUDGMENT   SIT   COURT   TAKEN

Cut and print! You did great! Now write your verse out on the lines below, and don't forget to practice this verse three times today!

_____

_____

_____

DAY TWO

A CLOSE-UP OF THE BEASTS

Yesterday as we zoomed in on Daniel 7:15-18, we got a glimpse of Daniel's distressed and alarmed spirit and discovered that the four beasts in his dream are four kings who will arise from the earth. HOW do these four kings and their kingdoms compare to the four kingdoms we saw represented on the statue in Daniel 2? Let's find out. Let's do a close-up on these four beasts.

"Okay, Mr. Grayson, get your camera ready," called Aunt

Sherry. "We're going to need some close-ups so we can find out what kingdoms these four beasts represent."

Don't forget to talk to God. Now read Daniel 7:3-8. Answer the 5 W's and an H below to help Mr. Grayson get a close-up shot of each beast.

Look at Daniel 7:4. WHAT was the first beast?

"It was like a _____ and had the _____ of an

_____.…. its wings were _____, and it was

_____ up from the ground and made to stand

on two feet like a _____; a _____ _____

also was given to it."

Did you know that the lion is often called the king of the beasts and symbolizes supremacy, power, and strength? In the Bible, the prophet Jeremiah in Jeremiah 49:19-22 used both the lion and eagle to refer to King Nebuchadnezzar. Pretty cool, huh?

Now think about the eagle's wings being plucked. Do you remember in our first season of Daniel how God humbled King Nebuchadnezzar and took away his rulership for seven periods of time in Daniel 4? Could Nebuchadnezzar's loss of his kingdom for seven periods of time be like the eagle's wings being plucked?

Think about this beast being lifted from the ground and made to stand like a man, and being given a human mind. Could this be when Nebuchadnezzar's reason returned to him and his kingdom was given back after he was a beast in the field? Amazing! Just think about all that you're learning. You're comparing Scripture with Scripture!

WHAT part of the statue on page 18 would this beast that is like a lion with the wings of an eagle represent? And WHAT is the name of this kingdom?

The h __ __ __ of g __ __ __ —the kingdom of

_____

Now turn to page 159. We have drawn pictures of the four beasts at the top of this page. Color the four beasts and carefully cut them out. (Don't cut out the goat and ram pictures yet.) Turn to your chart on page 18. In the column for Daniel 7, glue the picture of the lion next to the part of the statue in Daniel 2 it represents.

Way to go! Now look at Daniel 7:5. WHAT was the second beast like?

It was like a _____. "It was raised up on one

side, and _____ _____ were in its _____

between its _____."

WHAT can we learn about the bear? Is it as strong as a lion? _____

Did we see a kingdom on the statue that would be weaker (inferior) to King Nebuchadnezzar's kingdom? Look at your picture of the statue and read what you have written. WHAT part of the statue was inferior to King Nebuchadnezzar's?

The b __ __ __ __ __ and a __ __ __ of s __ __ __ __ __ __,

which represents the kingdom of the _____

and _____

Did you notice that the bear is raised on one side? This shows us that one part of this kingdom would be stronger than the other. Did you know that the Persians were dominant over the Medes? Does this fit in with the bear?

Glue the picture of the bear on your chart on page 18 next to the part of the statue it represents.

Daniel 7:6 WHAT is the third beast like?

It is "like a _____ which had on its back _____

_____ of a _____; and the beast had _____

_____, and _____ was given to it."

Now what do we know about leopards? We know they are very "fast cats." This one also has four wings on its back, which means this beast is a very, very fast cat! At this time, the Bible hasn't told us WHO the third kingdom is on our statue, but from looking at the animal we know this king will be fast like a leopard when he takes over and will have four heads.

Since we don't know the name of this kingdom yet, write out the part of the statue this leopard with four wings represents. WHAT part of the statue comes after the breast and arms of silver?

The b_ _ _ y and t _ _ _ _ s of b _ _ _ _ _

Glue the picture of the leopard on your chart on page 18 next to the part of the statue it represents.

Daniel 7:7-8 WHAT was the fourth beast like?

It was _____ and _____ and

extremely _____. It had large _____ teeth.

It _____ and _____ and _____ down

the remainder with its _____. It was _____

from all the beasts.

It had _____ h _ _ _ _. Another _____ , a

l _ _ _ _ _ o _ _, came up among them.

Wow—WHAT a beast! Since this beast is different than the others and doesn't have an animal description, we will call him "D.T." for *dreadful* and *terrifying*. Do you see any part of the statue that is made of iron? How about a part that has ten toes? This beast has how many horns? _____ horns

On WHAT part of the statue would you place this beast?

The l _ _ s of _____, and its f _ _ t of partly _____ and partly of _____

Glue the picture of the "D.T." beast on your chart on page 18 next to the part of the statue it represents.

All right! Isn't it awesome to see how God uses these dreams and visions to show us what is going to happen in the future? God gave Nebuchadnezzar the dream of an awesome statue, which gave the big picture of four kingdoms that would rule on earth.

God has fast-forwarded Daniel into the future to not only give him the big picture using beasts to describe these four kingdoms, but He also gives us details on this fourth kingdom.

We know who the first two kingdoms are. WHO are these other two kingdoms? WHAT makes this fourth kingdom dreadful and terrifying? Do you wonder what those "ten horns" represent? Think—have you seen another *ten* anywhere? Hang in there. We'll find out.

Keep up the good work. We are so proud of you!

DAY THREE

Lights, Camera, Action...

Didn't you have fun yesterday as you helped Mr. Grayson with his close-up shots of the four beasts and discovered where they fit with the dream of the statue? We can't wait to see this episode after Miss Lenyer adds in all those cool special effects. Those beasts aren't like anything we have ever seen before!

Today as we continue filming, we need to uncover the meaning of the rest of Daniel's vision, especially that "little horn" with eyes like a man and a mouth of boastful words. Have you ever heard of a horn like that? We better get to work.

"Quiet on the set. Don't forget to pray. Now count it down... and lights, camera, action!"

Read Daniel 7:19-28 on page 174 and mark your scripts with the key words listed in the box on the next page.

Key Words for Daniel 7:19-28

Daniel (color it blue)

fourth beast (color it brown)

different from all the others (color it pink)

ten horns (color it orange)

other horn (horn, another) (color it red)

I kept looking (circle it in blue)

saints (draw a blue star of David)

Ancient of Days (Highest One, Most High) (draw a purple triangle and color it yellow)

kingdom (draw a purple crown and color it blue)

Don't forget to mark your pronouns! And mark anything that tells you WHEN by drawing a green clock or green circle like this: .

WHAT things did Daniel want to know in verses 19-20?

Daniel 7:19 The meaning of the _____ _____

Daniel 7:20 The meaning of the _____ _____ and the _____ _____

Look back at Daniel 7:19. WHAT do we learn about the fourth beast?

It is _____ from the _____.

"It is exceedingly _____, with its _____
of _____ and its _____ of _____.

It d__ __ __ __ __ __ __ __, _____ and _____
down the _____ with its _____."

Daniel 7:20 WHAT do we learn about the "other horn"?

The other horn which _____ up, and before which _____ of them _____, that horn had _____ and a _____ uttering great _____ and was _____ in appearance than its associates.

Daniel 7:21 WHAT did Daniel see the horn doing?

_____

WHO is winning?

_____

WHOM does the horn overpower?

_____

Daniel 7:22 Until WHEN?

_____

WHAT happens after the judgment?

_____

Daniel 7:23 WHAT does Daniel find out about the fourth beast?

_____

_____

_____

_____

Daniel 7:24 WHAT or WHO are the ten horns? Hang on—here it comes straight from God! The ten horns are

_____ _____.

WHAT or WHO is the other horn that arises after the ten? He's called another WHAT? Another k __ __ __

Fantastic! Just look at what you discovered today. You know the fourth beast will be different than the kingdoms that come before it. This kingdom (the fourth) will devour, crush, and trample all of the other kingdoms. Out of this fourth kingdom will come ten kings with another king who will subdue three kings, just like you read in Daniel 7:8. He will also utter great boasts and wage war with the saints of the Highest One.

WHAT else will this king do? We'll find out tomorrow as we zoom in and get a close-up on this other horn. Don't forget to practice your memory verse. See you on the set tomorrow.

Day Four

A Close-up of the Little Horn

"Hey, guys, are you ready to help get a close-up of the 'little horn' in Daniel 7?" Aunt Sherry asked Max and Molly.

"We sure are!" Molly answered. "Will we find out WHO the 'little horn' is?"

Aunt Sherry laughed. "Of course we will, but," she paused and smiled, "not today."

"Oh, you're so bad, Aunt Sherry," Max responded. "The suspense is killing me. God must really love mysteries because He sure gives them in the Bible." Molly and Aunt Sherry both cracked up laughing. "Hang in there, you two. Studying the Bible takes time. And God doesn't always answer all our questions all at once, but He does show us the things He wants us to know. So let's get started. Max, why don't you ask God to give us patience and to reveal the things He wants us to know?"

"Sure, Aunt Sherry."

All right! Now that you've prayed, pull out your script and look at each place that you marked *another horn, little horn,* and *other horn* in Daniel 7. Let's get a close-up on this very important horn by making a list of everything we learn about it. Read Daniel 7 and get the details by filling in the chart below.

The Little Horn

Daniel 7:8 Came up among the t __ __ horns. Three of

the_____ horns were _____ out by the _____

before it. This horn possessed _____ like the

_____ of a _____ and a _____ uttering

great _____.

Daniel 7:20 _____ in appearance than its _____

Daniel 7:21 The horn was _____ _____ with the

_____ and _____ them.

Daniel 7:24 This horn is a k __ __ __ that will arise after

the ten kings. He will be _____ from the other

kings and he will subdue _____ _____.

Daniel 7:25 He will speak out _____ the _____

_____ and will wear down the _____ of the

_____ _____. He will intend to make

_____ in _____ and in _____.

The saints will be given into his hands for a _____,

_____, and _____ a _____.

Daniel 7:26 His _____ will be _____ away,

_____ and _____ forever.

Whoa! WHAT do you think about this "little horn" that's going to be a king? Did you notice in Daniel 7:20 the "little horn" becomes a big horn? Doesn't he sound awful? He speaks out against the Most High and wages war with His people and tries to change time and law. WHO do you think the Most High is? It's God, isn't it? This horn is in direct rebellion against God! Can you believe that? We also saw that the saints are given into this horn's hand for "time, times, and half a time."

Do you know how long "time, times, and half a time" is? This is a very important time phrase that we will see over and over again, as well as the time phrases 1260 days and 42 months. The biblical calendar only has 360 days instead of 365 days, so these time phrases of 42 months, 1260 days, and "time, times, and half a time" are different ways of saying the same amount of time. They are all a period of 3½ years. So the saints will be given into this little horn's hand for 3½ years!

Do you have any idea WHO this "little horn" could be? We'll find out more about him later. Just remember, no matter how bad he is, his dominion is taken away. He

is annihilated and destroyed forever! God is still in control. God gives this vision to His people, the sons of Israel, to give them hope. Yes, hard times are coming, but God is on His throne.

> Look at Daniel 7:27. WHO is given the sovereignty, dominion, and the greatness of all the kingdoms under the whole heaven?

> _____

> HOW long will His kingdom last?

> _____

> WHAT will everyone do?

> _____ and _____ Him

> Daniel 7:28 HOW did Daniel feel when the revelation ended?

> _____

Wow! No matter how bad things get, we have to remember that God's kingdom is the only one that will last forever. God is in control over all our circumstances. Nothing catches Him by surprise. Aren't you glad? God knows exactly what is going to happen tomorrow. That's why we need to put our trust in Him. You have done an awesome job!

Now say your memory verse out loud to remind you that the little horn's dominion will be taken away, that he will be annihilated and destroyed forever! All right!

DAY FIVE

A CHANGE OF SCENE

"Come on over," Miss Leslie called out. "Today we are going to see something incredible! We are going to tie Daniel to the Book of Revelation! Doesn't that sound awesome? We are going to take our Bibles and fast-forward over to Revelation to compare what we learned in Daniel 7 to the beast in Revelation 13. Remember, it's important for us to study the whole Bible and compare Scripture with Scripture because Scripture is the best interpreter of Scripture. Isn't that amazing? Our God is so awesome."

"He sure is!" Max said as he climbed up in his director's chair. "Uh-oh. Where's Sam?"

"There he is," Molly called out. "He's over there trying to help Mr. Andy get ready for the next scene."

Max called Sam. "Come on, boy, come on. Look, here's a treat. Come help us instead of Mr. Andy." Sam saw the treat in Max's hand and made a beeline for Max, jumping around in circles, eager to earn his treat.

Okay, now that Sam is back and happily eating his treat, we are ready to get started. Ask God for His help. Then pull out your Bible. Look up and read Revelation 13:1-7. Fill in your chart by comparing Scripture with Scripture. Fill in the blanks for Revelation 13:1-7. Then look at the next column and fill in the blanks for Daniel 7 to compare Daniel 7 to Revelation 13.

REVELATION 13

Revelation 13:1 The beast came up out of the _____, has _____ horns and _____ heads, and on his horns were ___ _____, and on his heads were _____ _____.
Did you know that diadems are crowns? Could ten diadems=ten kings?

Revelation 13:2 The beast was like a _____, his feet like a _____, and his mouth like a _____.
The dragon gave the beast his _____ and his _____ and great _____.

Revelation 13:5 There was given to him a _____ speaking _____ _____ and _____ and authority to act for _____ - _____ months.
Remember, 42 months and "time, times, and half a time" are all the same amount of time, 3½ years!

Revelation 13:6 He opened his _____ in _____ against _____.

Revelation 13:7 It was given to him to make _____ with the _____ and to _____ them.

DANIEL 7

Daniel 7:3 Four great beasts came out of the _____.

Daniel 7:7 The fourth beast had _____ horns.

Daniel 7:24 The ten horns are _____ k __ __ __ s.

Daniel 7:4-6 The first beast was like a _____, the second resembling a _____, the third like a _____, and _____ was given to it.

Daniel 7:8 This horn posessed _____ like the _____ of a man and a _____ uttering great _____.
Daniel 7:25 The saints will be given into his hand for a _____, _____, and _____ _____ _____.

Daniel 7:25 He will _____ out _____ the _____ _____.

Daniel 7:21 The horn was waging _____ with the _____ and _____ them.

Could this beast in Revelation be the "little horn" of Daniel 7? We'll have to keep studying to find out for sure. Isn't it incredible to see how the Bible all fits together? That's why it is so important to compare Scripture with Scripture!

You may not have all the answers, but you have learned some very important facts about this beast in Revelation and have made some awesome comparisons to the "little horn" in Daniel 7. There is so much more you can learn in Revelation about this beast and God's plan for the future. Max and Molly have two cool adventures on the Book of Revelation called *Bible Prophecy for Kids* and *A Sneak Peek into the Future*. You may want to do those after you finish Daniel.

Now go back and find all the words from each of the blanks in the chart and circle them in the word search below. Because we are comparing Scripture with Scripture, there will be words that are used more than one time. You only need to find and circle each word one time in the word search.

Y	E	A	G	A	I	N	S	T	E	S	G	N	I	K
Y	Y	F	E	F	M	O	U	T	H	N	S	A	H	W
T	E	K	K	S	Y	M	O	B	I	A	T	Z	N	I
K	S	A	I	N	T	S	M	R	J	R	S	J	O	T
K	E	E	S	I	M	E	H	P	S	A	L	B	H
D	M	P	H	A	R	W	H	I	A	M	O	W	L	R
O	A	S	A	B	O	U	P	B	D	E	B	H	R	O
M	N	D	R	P	H	M	S	G	E	D	M	G	S	N
I	G	L	R	O	T	H	A	L	F	A	T	I	M	E
N	U	E	O	W	U	E	L	T	Y	I	R	H	T	L
I	V	O	G	E	A	D	B	E	G	D	K	T	I	D
O	B	P	A	R	G	F	A	N	E	V	E	S	M	K
N	D	A	N	O	I	L	O	V	E	R	C	O	M	E
F	O	R	T	Y	T	W	O	Y	G	T	I	M	E	S
D	G	D	W	O	R	D	S	C	G	K	D	F	K	G

Hang in there! You are doing great! You are going to know God's plan for the future. Way to go! Don't forget to say your memory verse out loud to a grown-up this week.

3

A VISION OF A RAM AND A GOAT

DANIEL 8

Can you believe all we discovered last week in Daniel 7, as we started filming and zoomed in on Daniel's vision of the four beasts and the Ancient of Days? Were you amazed as you saw how each one of those beasts matched up with the kingdoms in the dream God gave King Nebuchadnezzar of the statue? How about how the beast in Revelation compares to the "little horn"? God is so incredible! He has all the pieces of the puzzle, and He lovingly reveals His plan to us. Unbelievable! Just think how cool it is that you are a kid and God would show you all this!

Today we are going to head back to the set to uncover WHAT happens in our new episode on Daniel 8. Will it be as exciting as Daniel 7? Will we discover WHO the third kingdom is? Let's find out.

DAY ONE

SCENE ONE: THE GOAT TRAMPLES THE RAM

"Oh, wow, Aunt Sherry!" Molly exclaimed as they came out of the screening room. "Miss Lenyer did an awesome job with the special effects. I can't get over how awesome and real those four beasts looked."

"How about that 'little horn' with those eyes and mouth?" Max asked. "But I loved the part with the 'Ancient of Days.' That was unbelievable! It's so hard to imagine such a fantastic scene—especially the part with the 'little horn' being annihilated and destroyed."

Aunt Sherry smiled. "Yes, just think: He went from being at the very top to ending up at the very bottom, annihilated and destroyed forever! That was an awesome scene. You guys have been such a great help. Before we get started on our new scene today, we need to review some of our background information on Daniel again because there is a change in the language in Daniel 8. Remember how we learned that Daniel was written in both the Hebrew and Aramaic languages? Molly, tell me again about Daniel 1."

"Okay. In Daniel 1 we saw God allow Jerusalem to be defeated by the Babylonians because of the sons of Israel's sin against God. Daniel 1 is written in Hebrew because it is about the sons of Israel, and Hebrew is the language of the Jewish people."

"You got it," Aunt Sherry replied. "Now it's your turn, Max."

"King Nebuchadnezzar captures the city of Jerusalem and takes Daniel and the sons of Israel into captivity to Babylon. In Daniel 2, Nebuchadnezzar dreams about a statue, which shows us four kingdoms, which are Gentile nations. Daniel 2–7 focuses on the Gentile nations, so it is written in Aramaic, which is the language of Nebuchadnezzar and the Gentile nations."

"Very good, guys. I am so proud of all your hard work. In Daniel 8, Daniel changes back to the Hebrew language because his audience changes. In Daniel 8–12, God changes the focus of His message from the Gentile nations, to show how these Gentile nations are going to affect His chosen people because of their sin against Him. These messages are for the Jewish people.

"Remember, God is a loving God, but because He is holy, He must deal with sin. In Daniel 8–12, God is going to fast-forward us into the future to show us what is going to happen to His chosen people (the Jews) to deal with their sin before the stone crushes the toes and Jesus comes back to set up His kingdom on earth."

"Wow!" Max exclaimed.

"Isn't that exciting," Aunt Sherry finished, "to see how the whole Book of Daniel fits together? Now that we have our background information, we are ready to shoot our next scene."

"We can't wait!" Max and Molly both yelled out, while Sam barked his agreement.

HOW did you do at remembering which language each chapter of Daniel was written in? Can you write it out below without looking?

Daniel 1 is written in _____.

Daniel ____ - ____ is written in _____.

Daniel ____ - ____ is written in _____.

Great! Are you ready to get started on Daniel 8?

Don't forget to ask God for His help in understanding His plan. Then pull out your script and turn to page 175. Read Daniel 8:1-7 and mark your key words listed in the box below on your Observation Worksheet. Add any new key words to your keyword bookmark.

Key Words for Daniel 8:1-7

Daniel (color it blue)

I looked (I lifted my eyes and I saw, I saw, etc.) (circle it in blue)

dream (vision) (draw a blue cloud around it)

ram (color it green)

goat (color it pink)

Don't forget to mark your pronouns! And mark anything that tells you WHERE by double-underlining the <u>WHERE</u> in green. Mark anything that tells you WHEN by drawing a green clock or green circle like this: ○ .

"Okay, places everyone," Aunt Sherry called out. "Olivia, check Daniel's costume. Now we're ready. Quiet on the set. Stand by. Roll Camera Two, Grayson. And action."

Daniel 8:1 WHEN is this happening?

_____

Look back at Daniel 7:1 on page 172. WHEN did Daniel 7 take place?

In the _____ year of Belshazzar's reign

Just to make sure you remember WHAT kingdom is in power at this time, WHAT kingdom is Belshazzar the king of?

The kingdom of _____

Since Daniel 7 happens in the first year of the reign of Belshazzar, and Daniel 8 opens in the third year of the reign of Belshazzar, we know that it has been two years since Daniel's vision of the four beasts. It is now 551 B.C., and Daniel would be somewhere around 70 years old. We're not really sure of his exact age.

Daniel 8:1 WHAT is happening?

Daniel has a _____.

Daniel 8:2 WHERE is Daniel in this vision?

_____

Daniel 8:3 WHAT does Daniel see?

_____

WHAT do we see about this ram?

_____

_____

_____

Daniel 8:4 WHAT did this ram do?

_____

_____

_____

Daniel 8:5 WHAT else did Daniel see?

_____

WHAT do we see about this goat?

_____

_____

_____

Daniel 8:6-7 WHAT happens? Draw a picture of this scene in the box on the next page.

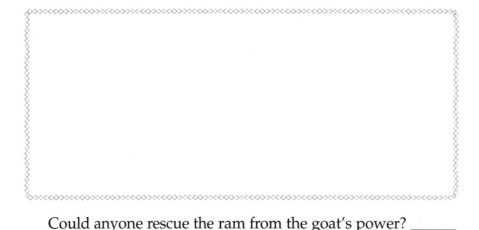

Could anyone rescue the ram from the goat's power? _____

Cut! WHAT an amazing vision! Do you have any idea WHAT this ram and goat represent? Guess what? Your new memory verse solves this mystery. We aren't going to let you discover your new memory verse today. You'll have to hang in there as we keep filming this cool episode to find out! But just to stay in practice, say one of your other memory verses today.

You'll find out more about this vision as we continue to shoot this exciting episode.

DAY TWO

SCENE TWO: THE GOAT MAGNIFIES HIMSELF

Yesterday you saw Daniel have another amazing vision about a ram and a goat. WHAT does this incredible vision mean? Grab your scripts and let's find out. Turn to page 176. Read Daniel 8:8-14 and mark the key words in the box below for these verses on your Observation Worksheet. Add any new key words to your key-word bookmark.

Key Words for Daniel 8:8-14

small horn (circle it in orange and color it red)

Beautiful Land (double-underline it in green and color it blue)

goat (color it pink)

Daniel (color it blue)

vision (draw a blue cloud)

Don't forget to mark your pronouns! And mark anything that tells you WHEN by drawing a green clock ⏲ or green circle like this: ◯ .

Now help Miss Lenyer as she plans how to create this scene's very cool special effects.

Daniel 8:8 WHAT did the male goat do?

_____

WHAT happened to his large horn?

_____

WHAT came up in its place?

_____

Daniel 8:9 WHAT came out of one of the four horns?

_____

List what you learn about this small horn in the box on the next page.

The Small Horn

Daniel 8:10 It grew up to the _____ of _____ and caused some of the _____ and some of the _____ to fall to the _____, and it _____ them down.

Daniel 8:11 It _____ itself to be _____ with the _____ of the _____; and it removed the _____ _____ from Him, and the place of His _____ was thrown down.

Daniel 8:12 The host will be given over to the _____ along with the _____ _____; and it will fling _____ to the ground and perform its _____ and _____.

Daniel 8:13 WHAT question did Daniel hear the holy one ask?

"How _____ will the _____ about the _____ _____ apply, while the _____ causes _____, so as to allow both the _____ _____ and the _____ to be _____?"

Daniel 8:14 HOW long will it be before the holy place is restored?

_____

Wow! Did you understand any of this vision? Yesterday we saw the goat trample the ram. After the goat defeats the ram, its large horn breaks and four horns come up, and out of one of the four comes a small horn, and Daniel hears a holy one ask a question.

WHAT are these four horns? Is this small horn the same as the little horn in Daniel 7? Hang in there! We'll find out. Don't forget to practice one of your memory verses. Tomorrow we will solve the mystery of the ram and the goat.

DAY THREE

SCENE THREE: GABRIEL REVEALS THE VISION

"All right! Max, why don't you and Molly check and see if Mr. Jackson is ready in makeup and Miss Olivia with the costumes? We'll be ready to shoot in about five minutes."

"Sure will, Aunt Sherry," Max replied as he and Molly headed to the makeup and costumes room. Max smiled at Molly. "I can't wait to see how Aunt Sherry films this scene that shows the meaning of Daniel's vision."

"Me, too," Molly answered. "I can't wait to see what the ram and the goat represent."

HOW about you? Are you ready to discover the meaning of Daniel's vision? Don't forget to pray! Turn to page 177. Read Daniel 8:15-22 and mark your key words in the box below or use your bookmark. Just don't forget to add any new key words to your bookmark.

Key Words for Daniel 8:15-22

Gabriel (color it yellow)

time of the end (the final period of indignation) (circle it in green and color it red)

Daniel (color it blue)

vision (draw a blue cloud)

ram (color it green)

goat (color it pink)

kingdom (draw a purple crown and color it blue)

Don't forget to mark your pronouns! And mark anything that tells you WHERE by double-underlining the WHERE in green. Mark anything that tells you WHEN by drawing a green clock or green circle like this: ◯ .

Daniel 8:15-16 WHO is going to help Daniel understand his vision?

_____

Daniel 8:17 WHEN does Gabriel tell Daniel what the vision pertains to?

The _____ of the _____

Daniel 8:19 WHAT is Gabriel going to let him know?

"What will occur at the _____ _____ of the

_____, for it pertains to the _____

_____ of the _____"

Daniel 8:20 WHOM does God say the ram represents?

_____

Now let's have fun. Let's compare this ram to what we have already seen in Daniel. Let's compare Scripture with Scripture by looking at the chart on the ram on page 61.

WHO IS THE RAM?

DANIEL 2	DANIEL 5	DANIEL 7	DANIEL 8
Think about the statue. Think about WHAT the ram represents. WHAT part of the statue is this? _____ _____ _____ _____	Daniel 5:28-31 WHO do we know conquered Babylon? The kingdom of the _____ and the _____	Think about the bear in Daniel 7:5. WHAT did we learn about the bear? It was _____ up on one _____ and _____ r __ __ s were in its _____ .	Think about the ram in Daniel 8:3. One horn on the ram was l _ _ _ _ _ than the other. Daniel 8:4 HOW many directions did the ram butt in? _____ Think: a lopsided bear, and a longer horn on the ram; three ribs in the bear's mouth, and three directions the ram butted in. Both the bear and the ram give us a picture of the second kingdom: the Kingdom of the _____ and the_____— the breast and arms of silver on the statue.

After you finish your chart on the ram, turn to page 159. Color and cut out the pictures of the ram and goat. Then turn to page 18 to your chart on Daniel's visions. Glue your ram in the last column under Daniel 8 next to the bear that represents the kings of Media and Persia.

Look at Daniel 8:21. WHOM does the shaggy goat represent?

_____

WHO is the large horn?

_____

Daniel 8:22 WHAT do the four horns represent that rise up in place of the broken horn?

_____

Just look at what you have discovered. God has just shown you the next kingdom! Now let's compare this goat to what we have already seen in Daniel. Fill in the chart on the goat.

WHO IS THE GOAT?

DANIEL 2	DANIEL 7	DANIEL 8
Think about the statue. Now we know the goat trampled the ram. So WHAT part of the statue comes after the ram (the kingdom of the Medes and Persians)? The b _ _ _ y and _____ of _____	Daniel 7:6 WHAT do we see about the leopard? On its back it had _____ _____ of a bird, it had _____ heads, and dominion was given to it.	Daniel 8:5 The goat was coming from the west over the _____ of the whole _____ without _____ at the _____. Daniel 8:8 The large horn breaks and in its place there came up ____ horns.

So WHERE would this goat go on our chart of Daniel's visions? Think about what we just saw as we compared these passages of Scripture. Think about the leopard in Daniel 7. It has four wings on its back and four heads. This is a very, very fast cat. Look at how the goat moved so fast over the surface of the whole earth that its feet don't touch the ground. It sounds pretty fast, too! And the goat has a large horn that breaks, with four horns that come after it.

The goat had four horns and the leopard had four heads and four wings, and they are both very, very fast. Do these two animals sound like they represent the same kingdom?

We also saw that the goat tramples the ram. So the goat's kingdom must come after the ram's. Glue the picture of your goat in its correct place on your chart on Daniel's visions on page 18.

Daniel 8:21 WHO did the goat represent?

The kingdom of G __ __ __ __ __

Look at the picture of your statue and write next to the belly and thighs of bronze the name of this third kingdom, the kingdom of Greece.

Isn't it awesome how God fills in the details on what is going to happen in the future? Take a look below at the notes of Miss Anna, the production manager, to see what you can learn about this third kingdom.

 **PRODUCTION MANAGER'S NOTES**

THE KINGDOM OF GREECE

The kingdom of Greece began in 331 B.C. Alexander the Great (the first king, the large horn on the goat) conquered the Medes and the Persians at the age of 33 years old. One of the amazing facts is how quickly Alexander conquered the entire Medo-Persian kingdom. It was so fast that some scholars have said, "He touched not the ground." (Remember our leopard and goat.)

Alexander dies suddenly (the broken large horn), and since

*there is no appointed heir, four of his generals eventu-
ally divide his kingdom. Think about those four heads on
the leopard in Daniel 7 and the four horns on the goat in
Daniel 8 that represent four kingdoms.*

*Alexander's empire is divided with 1. Lysimachus
taking Thrace and Bithynia, 2. Cassander
taking Macedonia, 3. Ptolemy I Soter taking
Egypt, and 4. Seleucus I Nicator taking Syria.*

Pretty amazing! Did you know that National Geographic has a video on Alexander the Great? At our present time in history, all three of these kingdoms have come and gone. Did you know that Daniel had this vision before there was a second kingdom? At the time Daniel receives the vision in Daniel 8, there is only one kingdom, the Babylonian kingdom.

In Daniel 5:31 we see the Medes and Persians take over the kingdom of Babylon, but at this time in Daniel 8 it is 12 years before Babylon is taken in Daniel 5. And since Greece doesn't defeat the Medes and Persians until 331 B.C., Daniel will not live to see this third kingdom.

God has given Daniel an awesome glimpse into the future. Isn't that exciting? WHAT about the rest of Daniel's vision about the "small horn"? WHO is this "small horn" in Daniel 8, and is it the same as the "little horn" or "another horn" in Daniel 7? We'll find out.

Now before you leave the set today, you need to solve this week's memory verse about the ram and the goat.

To solve the mystery of this verse, you need to decide which of the missing vowels (a, e, i, o, u) needs to go on each of the blanks on the next page. Once you have added the vowels to the blanks and solved the mystery, find the reference that goes with this verse. Then run Gabriel's lines, practice saying this verse aloud, three times in a row, three times today.

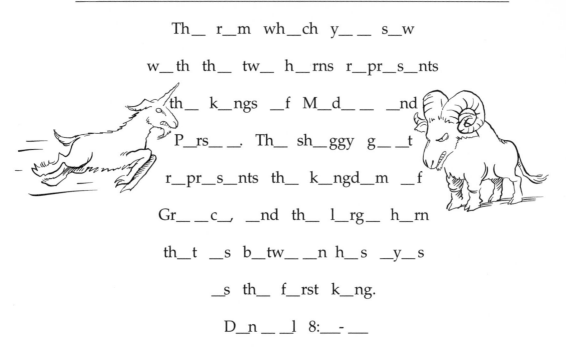

Th_ r_m wh_ch y_ _ s_w

w_ th th_ tw_ h_rns r_pr_s_nts

th_ k_ngs _f M_d_ _ _nd

P_rs_ _. Th_ sh_ggy g_ _t

r_pr_s_nts th_ k_ngd_m _f

Gr_ _ c_, _nd th_ l_rg_ h_rn

th_t _s b_tw_ _n h_s _y_s

_s th_ f_rst k_ng.

D_n _ _l 8:_ - _

You did it! Now practice saying these verses three times today, so that you will remember what you learned about the ram and the goat.

DAY FOUR

SCENE FOUR: A KING RISES

"Hey, Aunt Sherry," Molly called out as she walked across the set with Max, "are we going to film the scene with the small horn today?"

"We sure are. It's a pretty sad scene when you see what is going to happen to Israel, God's chosen people. Why don't you and Max pull out your scripts and mark this last scene in Daniel 8?"

"Let's get started. I'll pray," Max volunteered.

Are you ready? Then grab your script and turn to page 178. Read Daniel 8:23-27 and mark your key words for these last verses on your Observation Worksheet. Add any new key words to your bookmark.

Key Words for Daniel 8:23-27

king (circle it in orange and color it red)

destroy (draw a black jagged line like this: ⚡)

Daniel (color it blue)

vision (draw a blue cloud)

Don't forget to mark your pronouns! And mark anything that tells you WHEN by drawing a green clock 🕐 or green circle like this: ◯ .

"Okay, places everybody. We're ready to roll. Quiet on the set. Stand by...action."

Look back at Daniel 8:21-22. Remember, the broken horn is the first king (Alexander the Great) from the kingdom of Greece. And we saw that in his place (when the horn breaks) there will be four kingdoms. In Daniel 8:23 it says "in the latter period of their rule." WHOSE rule is this? It's the rule of the four kingdoms, the four horns that come out of the broken horn.

Daniel 8:23 WHAT will happen in the latter period of their rule (the four kingdoms)?

A _____ will _____.

WHERE does this king that will arise come from? Think about what we just learned in Daniel 8:21-23. This king that will arise comes out of the f__ __ __ k __ __ __ __ __ __ __ .

And WHAT kingdom do the four come out of? WHAT kingdom does the goat represent? The kingdom of G _ _ _ _ _

Daniel 8:24 WHAT do we learn about this king?

_____

_____

Daniel 8:25 WHAT will he do in his heart?

He will _____ himself.

WHAT will he do to those at ease?

_____

WHOM will he oppose?

_____

WHAT will happen to him?

_____

Daniel 8:26 WHAT does Daniel find out about the vision?

_____

WHAT is he told to do?

_____

WHY? _____

Daniel 8:27 HOW did Daniel feel? WHAT did he do?

_____

_____

Cut! You got an awesome shot of Daniel's face. Think about how he reacted to this vision. WHO is this horrible king that will destroy the holy people? We'll take a closer look at him tomorrow.

A CLOSE-UP OF THE KiNG

Yesterday as we filmed our final scene in Daniel 8 we got a glimpse of a very horrible king in Daniel 8:23-27. WHO is this horrible king? Is this king the "small horn" we saw in Daniel 8:8-14? Let's find out. Don't forget to talk to God.

Now look at the chart below. Let's compare the "small horn" in Daniel 8:8-14 to the king that arises in Daniel 8:23-27.

Small Horn	The King That Arises
Daniel 8:8 WHAT comes out of the large broken horn? _____ horns	Daniel 8:22 WHAT comes out of the broken horn? _____ horns WHAT do the four horns represent? _____ _____
Daniel 8:8-9 WHAT comes out of the four horns? A rather _____ horn	Daniel 8:22-23 WHAT comes out of the four kingdoms? A _____ will arise.
Daniel 8:11 It _____ itself to be equal with the _____ of the _____ .	Daniel 8:25 He will _____ himself in his _____ .

Now that you have compared these passages of Scripture, is the small horn in Daniel 8:9 the same as the king in Daniel 8:23? _____

Yes he is. This king comes out of the four horns which are four kingdoms, just like the "small horn" comes out of four horns in Daniel 8:8-9. The "small horn" is the king in Daniel 8:23.

So now that we know that this king is the small horn in Daniel 8, is this "small horn" the same as the "little horn" in Daniel 7? HOW can we find out? You should know by now. Let's compare the "small horn" in Daniel 8 to the "little horn" in Daniel 7. Fill in the chart below.

Small Horn in Daniel 8	Little Horn in Daniel 7
Daniel 8:8-9 WHAT animal is the small horn on? The _____	Daniel 7:7-8 WHAT animal is the little horn on? The f _ _ _ _ _ beast, which we call the " ___. ___." beast.
WHAT kingdom is this? The kingdom of G _ _ _ _ _, which is the t_ _ _ d kingdom	WHAT kingdom does this beast represent? The f _ _ _ _ _ kingdom.
Daniel 8:8-9 This horn comes out of _____ horns.	Daniel 7:7-8 This horn comes out of _____ horns.

Are these two horns the same? No. They come from two different kingdoms. The "small horn" is a king that will come out of **four horns** from the **third kingdom** of Greece. The "little horn" is a king that comes out of the **fourth kingdom** and who will rise up after the **ten horns** (the ten kings) and subdue three of the kings.

Amazing! Aren't you excited that you discovered this all by yourself by comparing Scripture with Scripture? Is there a king in history that would fit this description of the small horn from the kingdom of Greece? Check out Miss Anna's research on the next page!

PRODUCTION MANAGER'S NOTES

ANTIOCHUS IV EPIPHANES

The small horn in Daniel 8 was a king named Antiochus IV Epiphanes who ruled Syria from 171 B.C. to 165 B.C.

Antiochus added the name EPIPHANES to his name because it meant "God manifested." He magnified himself to be equal with God! Wow, he sure thought an awful lot about himself! In Daniel 8:11, God showed Daniel there would be a small horn who magnified himself to be equal with Commander of the host. Amazing!

In 171 B.C., Antiochus IV Epiphanes goes to Jerusalem. When he gets there, he goes inside the temple and into the holy of holies. Did you know that only the high priest was allowed into the holy of holies inside the temple, and he could only go in one time a year to make atonement for sin? Antiochus IV Epiphanes not only goes inside the holy of holies, but he also puts up a statue of the pagan Greek god Zeus, desecrating God's temple.

Every day the priest in the temple would sacrifice a lamb two times a day, once in the morning and once in the evening, along with a flour and oil offering. Antiochus IV Epiphanes not only stops this regular offering, but he also sacrifices a pig on the altar. A pig was an unclean animal for the Jews. Remember, God's people were told what animals were clean to eat and sacrifice. Antiochus IV Epiphanes stopped the daily sacrifices for 2300 mornings and evenings until December 25, 165 B.C. Unbelievable!

Take a look at Daniel 8:14. HOW long did it say it would be until the holy place was properly restored?

_____

HOW long did Antiochus IV Epiphanes stop the regular sacrifices?

_____

Incredible! Amazing! Awesome! God gave all the details about the small horn that are fulfilled in Antiochus IV Epiphanes before it ever happened! Antiochus IV Epiphanes wasn't even on the horizon at the time of Daniel's vision. God showed Daniel exactly what would happen to his people. That's our awesome God!

Look at how Daniel reacted. He was exhausted and sick for days. Daniel was heartbroken over the hard things he knew were coming for his people, but he trusted God's plan. Daniel got up and carried on the king's business. WHAT an incredible man! He trusted God, no matter what the circumstances.

HOW about you? Do you trust God when bad things happen to you? _____ Write out what you do when something bad happens. _____

The next time something bad happens, will you be like Daniel? Will you trust that God knows what is best, even when it doesn't look like it? Will you run to God and ask for His help? Write out WHAT you will do._____

You have done a fantastic job! Don't forget to say your memory verse to a grown-up. See you on the set next week!

4

A 70-WEEK PROPHECY

DANIEL 9

It's great to have you back! Wasn't it cool to see God give Daniel a second vision of a ram and goat that represented the second and third kingdoms? We also saw a small horn come out of one of the four horns on the head of the goat and discovered that the "small horn" was a very horrible king in the third kingdom of Greece named Antiochus IV Epiphanes. Antiochus IV Epiphanes was a very evil king who made himself to be equal with God. He did some horrible things to God's people. And we also found out that this "small horn" in Daniel 8 is not the "little horn" in Daniel 7. WHO is the "little horn" that comes out of the fourth kingdom? God hasn't shown us yet. Will He? Hang on! Let's head back to the set to find out WHAT happens next.

DAY ONE

SCAN THE SCRIPT!

"Sam, where are you, boy?" Max called as he and Molly walked around the set peeking into rooms looking for Sam. "Hey, Molly, I found him. Come over here quick! You have to see him.

He's sitting in Miss Olivia's dressing room, and she has him all dressed up."

Molly peeked her head in the door and started laughing. "Sam, old boy, what will you get into next?" Miss Olivia smiled. "I saw him sniffing around the costumes, so I thought I'd dress him up. Why don't you take him over to Grayson and let him get a picture for you?"

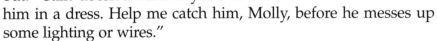

"Uh-oh, there he goes," Max called out. "Sam doesn't want anyone to see him in a dress. Help me catch him, Molly, before he messes up some lighting or wires."

"Whew! We did it! Sam, you are such a bad dog, but you sure are a lot of fun! Come on, Molly, we need to go work on our scripts."

Now that Sam has been captured and gotten out of his girlie clothes, we need to pull out our scripts and get to work. Don't forget to talk to God. Now let's scan our scripts to find out WHAT is happening in Daniel 9. Turn to page 178. Read Daniel 9:1-2.

Daniel 9:1 WHEN is this happening?

In the _____ year of _____

WHO was Darius king over?

The _____ of the _____

Daniel 9 is taking place in the first year of King Darius's reign. Do you remember Darius the Mede receiving the kingdom at the end of chapter 5 when Belshazzar was slain? This is the beginning of the kingdom of the Medes and the Persians. We see the beginning of Darius the Mede's reign in Daniel 6. It is now 539 B.C. Daniel would be somewhere around 80 years old. Guess what? Even though Daniel is 80 years old, God's not through with him yet!

Daniel 9:2 WHAT did Daniel observe in the books?

"The _____ of the _____ which was revealed
as the word of the LORD to _____ the prophet for
the _____ of the _____ of Jerusalem,
namely, _____ years"

The word *desolations* means "ruined home" or "waste places."
It also means something that is uninhabited, deserted, or forsaken.
Daniel is reading about how long Jerusalem will be ruined and
uninhabited by God's nation Israel.

Is there any hope of Jerusalem being inhabited again by
God's people? Let's look up Jeremiah 29 to see WHAT Daniel
read about the desolations of Jerusalem.

Look up and read Jeremiah 29:1.

Jeremiah 29:1 WHOM does Jeremiah send a letter to?

"To the rest of the _____ of the exile, the _____, the
_____, and all the _____ whom Nebuchad-
nezzar had taken into _____ from Jerusalem to
Babylon."

Now read Jeremiah 29:10-14.

Jeremiah 29:10 HOW long does the Lord tell them they
will be in exile? _____ _____

WHAT will the Lord do when the 70 years have been
completed for Babylon?

"I will visit you and _____ My good word to you,
to _____ you back to this place."

Jeremiah 29:11 WHAT are the Lord's plans for His
people?

"Plans for _____ and not for _____ to give you
a _____ and a _____."

Jeremiah 29:12 WHAT does the Lord tell them to do?

"_____ upon Me and come and _____ to Me."

WHAT will God do?

"I will _____ to you."

Jeremiah 29:14 "I will be _____ by you…I will _____ your fortunes and will _____ you from all the nations and from all the places where I have driven you."

Now go back and find all the words from each of the blanks from the beginning of Daniel 9 on page 74 through Jeremiah 29 on page 76 and circle them in the word search below. If a word is used more than once, you only need to circle it one time.

D	E	S	O	L	A	T	I	O	N	S	N	A	V
N	R	E	J	S	T	E	H	P	O	R	P	F	T
U	O	V	N	C	F	U	L	F	I	L	L	C	E
O	T	E	L	D	E	R	S	P	T	G	H	S	H
F	S	N	F	U	T	U	R	E	E	A	U	K	G
N	E	T	V	Y	T	I	M	A	L	A	C	S	S
R	R	Y	G	Q	E	Y	J	D	P	N	D	E	W
M	R	N	A	S	K	E	E	E	M	E	P	Z	W
J	E	G	T	M	I	A	R	N	O	T	E	B	J
K	B	S	H	B	N	R	E	A	C	S	O	P	R
V	M	P	E	S	G	S	M	L	F	I	P	R	X
S	U	I	R	A	D	J	I	J	I	L	L	A	C
G	N	I	R	B	O	S	A	L	W	X	E	Y	N
T	S	R	I	F	M	Z	H	O	P	E	E	W	L

Wow! Daniel was reading God's Word about how long Israel would be in captivity. HOW long was it until God would bring them back to the land? HOW long until the completion of the desolations of Jerusalem? _____ years

That's a long time! But look at the hope God gives them. After the 70 years are up, God will bring them back to the land and restore their fortunes. God is a good and awesome God! God is faithful to His promises! He made a covenant with the nation of Israel, and He's going to keep it! God told His people that this land and this city would be theirs forever, and God always keeps His promises!

WHY would God send his people into captivity for 70 years? Do you know? We know God took the sons of Israel into captivity because they disobeyed Him. They sinned against God. We saw that when we filmed *You're a Brave Man, Daniel!* But we don't know WHY He let them get taken for 70 years. We'll find out tomorrow.

Before we leave the set, we need to discover this week's memory verse. Look at the teleprompter below. It looks like someone made a mistake when they fed Daniel's lines into the machine. They fed them in backwards.

You need to look at the first line of letters, starting on the far right, and write each letter from right to left on the first line below. Then you need to do the same thing for the next five lines of letters to unscramble this verse so that you can cue Daniel. Then look up Daniel 9 and find the reference for this verse.

> eht ni nettirw si ti sA
>
> ytimalac siht lla ,sesoM fo wal
>
> ton evah ew tey ;su no emoc sah
>
> ruo droL eht fo rovaf eht thguos
>
> ytiuqini ruo morf gninrut yb doG
>
> .hturt ruoY ot noitnetta gnivig dna

_____

_____

_____

_____

_____

_____

Daniel 9:_____

Great work!

BEHIND THE SCENES

"Come on in," Miss Leslie called out to Max and Molly. "Did Sherry tell you that today we are going behind the scenes to gather our background information to find out why God allowed the children of Israel to be taken into captivity seventy years?"

"Yes, she did," Molly replied.

"Good. Climb up in your chairs and pull out your scripts. We're going to look up different passages of Scripture. Max, why don't you pray, and then we can get to work?"

Now that we have talked to God, let's get started. Look up the verses of Scripture below and ask the 5 W's and an H to solve the crossword puzzle on page 79.

Look up and read Leviticus 25:1-7.

> Leviticus 25:1-2 WHAT did the Lord speak to Moses? WHAT did God tell the sons of Israel they were to do when they came into the land?
>
> 1. (Across) "The land shall have a _____ to the LORD."

> Leviticus 25:3 HOW long were they to sow their fields, prune their vineyards, and gather their crops?
>
> 2. (Across) _____ years

> Leviticus 25:4 WHAT were they to do in the seventh year?
>
> 3. (Down) The land shall have a sabbath _____.

A sabbath rest is a year when they would not sow their fields or prune their vineyards or reap their crops.

Now look up and read Leviticus 26:27-35.

Leviticus 26:27 WHAT were the children of Israel not doing?

4. (Across) They did not _____ God.

Leviticus 26:32 WHAT did God say He would do because they didn't obey?

5. (Down) "I will make the land _____."

Leviticus 26:33 WHAT would happen to the people?

6. (Across) "I will _____ you among the

7. (Down) _____."

Look up and read 2 Chronicles 36:20-23.

2 Chronicles 36:21 HOW long would they be in exile?

8. (Across) Until the _____ had enjoyed its

9. (Across) _____ and

10. (Down) until _____

11. (Down) _____ were complete.

Wow! During a time of 490 years, Israel had disobeyed God and not given the land its sabbath rest. Can you believe it? And because they owed God 70 sabbaths, God let them be taken into captivity for 70 years. Once again we see God means exactly what He says. He does not tolerate disobedience from His children.

The children of Israel were taken into captivity in 605 B.C., and it is now 539 B.C.

HOW long have they been in captivity?

_____

HOW long do they have before their 70 years are complete?

_____

Do you see how important it is for you to know God's Word and do what God says is right? James 4:17 says, *"Therefore, to one who knows the right thing to do and does not do it, to him it is sin."*

Ask yourself if you do the right thing or if you are sinning. For example, in Ephesians 6:1-2 God says we are to obey and honor our parents. Are you obeying your parents? Do you treat them with honor, or do you disrespect them with your words, your attitude, and your actions? Write on the line below WHAT you do. Tell if you know the right thing to do. Then tell HOW you obey or disobey your parents, as well as HOW you honor or disrespect them.

_____

_____

If you see anything you're doing wrong, go to God and ask Him for His help. Ask Him to forgive you for sinning and to help you do what is right. Way to go! We are so very proud of you! Tomorrow we will find out how Daniel reacts to the words of Jeremiah. Don't forget to practice your memory verse.

DAY THREE

QUIET ON THE SET

"Okay," Aunt Sherry called out, "quiet on the set. We're ready to open with Daniel reading the Book of Jeremiah. Grayson, open wide, then go in tight for a close-up on Daniel. And action."

How does reading Jeremiah's words affect Daniel? Let's find out. Turn to page 178. Read Daniel 9:1-19 and mark the key words listed in the box below on your Observation Worksheet for these verses. Add any new key words to your key-word bookmark.

Key Words for Daniel 9:1-19

Jerusalem (Your city, Your holy mountain) (box it in blue)

prayer (draw a purple ⌣ and color it pink)

Daniel (color it blue)

God (Lord) (draw a purple triangle and color it yellow)

we have sinned (sin) (color it brown)

kingdom (draw a purple crown and color it blue)

Don't forget to mark your pronouns! And mark anything that tells you WHERE by double-underlining the WHERE in green. Mark anything that tells you WHEN by drawing a green clock 🕐 or green circle like this: ○ .

Daniel 9:3 WHAT does Daniel do after reading Jeremiah's words?

_____

Daniel 9:4 WHAT does Daniel do in his prayer?

_____

Daniel 9:5 WHAT does Daniel confess they had done?

_____

_____

Daniel 9:6 WHAT had they not done?

_____

Make a list in the box below of all the things the children of Israel did in Daniel 9:7-16. We did the first one for you.

What the Children of Israel Did

Daniel 9:7 They committed unfaithful deeds against God.

Daniel 9:16 WHAT does Daniel ask God to do?

_____

Daniel 9:19 WHAT does Daniel ask God to do in this verse?

_____

Wow! Reading the Book of Jeremiah has a huge impact on Daniel. He is brokenhearted over the sins of his people and the desolations that have come upon them. Remember, they have been in captivity for 66 years, and Jerusalem is uninhabited by God's nation, Israel.

Look at what Daniel does. He gives his attention to the Lord and seeks Him in prayer and fasting. Daniel pleads for God's forgiveness for his people's wickedness and rebellion.

Do you have a sensitive heart when it comes to seeing sin in your life? Do you confess the things you do wrong and turn away from them? Remember what we learned when we looked at Jeremiah 29 on Day One: Call on God and pray, and God will listen to you. First John 1:9 tells us, *"If we confess our sins, He is faithful and righteous to forgive us our sins and to cleanse us from all unrighteousness."*

Be like Daniel! Seek God, admit your sin, and ask Him to cleanse you and help you to obey Him.

DAY FOUR

ZOOMiNG iN

Yesterday as we filmed our first scene in Daniel 9, we saw Daniel humble himself before God in sackcloth and ashes and confess all the things the sons of Israel had done. He pleads with God to hear his prayer, to see their desolations, to be compassionate and take action because Jerusalem is God's city and is called by God's name.

As Daniel prays, we see him praise God for WHO He is. Today we need to zoom in and take a close-up look at what we learn about God in Daniel 9:1-19. It's very important to know WHO God is, so we can praise Him the way He would want us to! Don't forget to talk to God!

Make a list of the things you learn about God in Daniel 9:4-19 in the box below.

What I'm Learning About God

God is a great and awesome God. He keeps His promises. He is righteous. He is lovingkindness. He gets angry. He sends calamity. He is compassionate and forgiving. He teaches us. What an amazing God!

Write out HOW God has been good to you.

_____

_____

_____

Now take a moment and thank God for WHO He is and all He has done for you. Write out a prayer to God.

_____

_____

_____

Don't forget to say your memory verse. Let this verse remind you to seek God's favor, to turn from your iniquity, and to give attention to God's truth. Fantastic! We are so proud of you!

DAY FiVE

SpECiAL EFFECTS

"Hey, guys, are you ready to help us shoot a scene that will have some very cool special effects?" Aunt Sherry asked. "Do you remember Ryan, our art director, and Justin, our stunt coordinator? They are working on our next scene. We're going to be using the blue screen again to film our characters. Remember, when a blue screen is used, only the characters are photographed by the camera. Later Miss Lenyer, the digital artist, will insert the characters into this scene using the computer to make it look like they are really there."

"Can we help Mr. Ryan and Mr. Justin?" Max asked.

"Sure! Why don't you finish marking your scripts, then you can help them?"

"That's a great idea, Aunt Sherry," Molly responded. "I'll pray, Max, and then we can mark our scripts."

Grab your script and turn to page 180. Read Daniel 9:20-27 and mark the key words on page 86 for these verses on your Observation Worksheet. Add any new key words to your bookmark.

Key Words for Daniel 9:20-27

Gabriel (color it yellow)

vision (draw a blue cloud around it)

Messiah (Messiah the Prince) (draw a purple cross and color it yellow)

(WHO is Messiah? Do you know? Take a minute to look up John 1:41-42 to make sure you know who Messiah is.)

prince who is to come (one who makes desolate) (color it red)

Jerusalem (Your holy city, the holy mountain) (box it in blue)

prayer (draw a purple ⌣ and color it pink)

Daniel (color it blue)

sin (color it brown)

God (Lord) (draw a purple triangle and color it yellow)

Don't forget to mark your pronouns! And mark anything that tells you WHEN by drawing a green clock 🕐 or green circle like this: ○.

"Okay, places everyone," Aunt Sherry called out. "Is Gabriel ready? Jackson, check Gabriel's makeup. All right. It looks good. Quiet on the set. Roll Camera Two, Grayson. And action."

Daniel 9:20-21 WHAT happened while Daniel was speaking, praying, and confessing his sin and the sin of his people?

_____ came to Daniel in his extreme _____ .

Daniel 9:22 WHAT is Gabriel going to give Daniel?

_____

Daniel 9:23 WHAT did Gabriel tell Daniel? HOW is Daniel thought of?

"You are _____ _____."

Wow! Wouldn't that be awesome to have an angel tell you that you are highly esteemed (precious) to God? Daniel was precious to God because he obeyed God.

Daniel 9:23 WHAT does Gabriel tell Daniel to do?

_____

That means to pay attention and to do what it says.

Daniel 9:24 HOW many weeks are there in this message?

_____ weeks

Are these literal weeks? In Daniel 9:24 the word for *weeks* literally is "sevens," therefore these 70 weeks are 70 sevens, which would be 70 x 7, which equals 490. Now would this be 490 hours, days, weeks, or years? Looking at the time frame in the Bible, we know that these events did not happen in hours, days, or weeks, so it has to be 490 years.

Let's find out WHAT Gabriel's message is. WHAT is going to happen during these 70 sevens or 490 years? Fill in the chart to find out.

The 70 Weeks of Daniel

Daniel 9:24 WHOM is the prophecy decreed for?

_____

Daniel 9:24 WHAT has to happen in these 70 weeks?

1. To _____ the _____

2. To make an _____ of _____

3. To make _____ for _____

4. To bring in _____ _____

5. To _____ up vision and _____

6. To _____ the most _____ _____

Daniel 9:26 WHAT will happen to the city and sanctuary?

_____

Daniel 9:27 WHAT are the events of the last week?

1. He will _____ a _____ _____

   with the _____ .

2. In the _____ of the week he will put a _____

   to_____ and _____ _____.

3. On the wing of _____ he will make

   _____.

HOW is the week divided?_____

WHAT is the length of each division? HOW would you split a week down the middle?

_____ ½ days and _____ ½ = seven days or one week

All right! You have just uncovered the facts about a very important prophecy. WHAT does it all mean? Hang in there! We'll find out next week as we do some background work for this very important episode. This isn't an easy prophecy to understand, but you can get it if you persevere!

Don't forget to say your memory verse to a grown-up this week. Ask this person if he or she is giving attention to the truth, God's Word.

Way to go!

5

A MAN DRESSED IN LINEN

DANIEL 9–10

As we began filming in Daniel 9 we saw Daniel humble himself before God, heartbroken over the sins of Israel and pleading with God for forgiveness. What an awesome man! No wonder Daniel is highly esteemed by God. The things that hurt God hurt Daniel. Sin always breaks God's heart. That's why you don't want to sin. You don't want to hurt God. Daniel always obeyed God, even if it meant ending up in the lions' den.

As Daniel prays, Gabriel comes to explain Daniel's vision of the 70 weeks that have been decreed for his people. WHAT does this very important prophecy mean? WHO is the "prince who is to come" who will make a firm covenant with the many? WHAT does the man dressed in linen say in Daniel 10? Let's head back to the set to find out. There is so much more to discover this week.

DAY ONE

BACKGROUND CHECK

"Hey, Miss Lenyer, you did an awesome job creating those special effects in the scene of Gabriel and Daniel," Molly told

Miss Lenyer as she, Max, and Miss Lenyer headed back to Aunt Sherry. "We had so much fun helping you out!"

"You guys did a great job! Are you ready to learn more about this awesome prophecy that God gives Daniel?"

"We sure are!" Max replied. "I can't wait to find out who this 'prince who is to come' is. He sounds pretty bad to me."

"You're right about that," said Miss Lenyer. "Okay, let's go grab our scripts. Before we can film the rest of this episode, we need to make sure we understand the events in this prophecy. I'll pray, and then we can get started on our background work."

All right! Now that you have talked to God, turn to page 181. Read Daniel 9:24 and look at the six things that you listed on your chart on page 88 that must happen in the 70 weeks for Daniel's people (the Jews) and the city of Jerusalem. Let's think about these six things. Have these six things taken place today?

1. Have the transgressions, the rebellious acts against God, by God's people (Israel) stopped yet?
   ___ Yes or ___No

2. Has there been an end to sin? (When these 70 weeks are finished there will be an end to sin.)
   ___ Yes or ___No

3. Has there been atonement, a pardon or forgiveness for sin? ___ Yes or ___ No

4. Has everlasting righteousness been brought in, has Israel quit sinning, and have they accepted Jesus as the Christ, the Messiah? ___ Yes or ___No

5. Has the vision been sealed up, completed? Has all of prophecy been fulfilled? ___ Yes or ___No

6. Has the holy place been anointed? Is there a temple now in Jerusalem? Has Jesus come back again?
   ___ Yes or ___No

WHAT did you write when you got to number 3? Stop and

think about number 3. Can a person have their sins forgiven?
_____

As you can see, when you go through each one of these six things, none of them has happened yet except number 3. When Jesus came the first time, when He died on the cross, He made atonement for our sins. He paid for our sins in full! So this has been fulfilled. The other five things haven't happened yet, but we know they will happen before the 70 weeks end.

WHEN do these 70 weeks begin? Have they already started? Let's find out.

Turn to page 181. Read Daniel 9:25-26.

WHEN do these 70 weeks begin?

Daniel 9:25 WHEN are they to begin?

From the _____ of a _____ to _____

and _____ _____ until _____

the _____

This verse shows us that the 70 weeks begin when there is a decree to restore and rebuild Jerusalem *until* Messiah the Prince. Did you know that *Messiah* is the Hebrew word for Christ? Remember, we saw that Jesus is called the Messiah. So we know that the decree to restore and rebuild Jerusalem had to happen before Jesus comes. Let's find out WHEN the decree happened.

Look up and read Nehemiah 2:1-8.

Nehemiah 2:1 WHO is king at this time?

_____

Nehemiah 2:5 WHAT did Nehemiah want to do?

_____

Nehemiah 2:7-8 Did the king grant permission to Nehemiah to go and rebuild the city? _____

In 445 BC, King Artaxerxes (the king of the Persians) issued a decree for Nehemiah to rebuild the wall and the city. So the prophecy of the 70 weeks started in 445 BC at the issuing of this decree to rebuild Jerusalem.

Turn to your timeline on page 117. Where it says "Decree to Rebuild Jerusalem," write "445 BC" in the blank.

> Daniel 9:25 HOW many weeks is it from the issuing of a decree to restore and rebuild Jerusalem until Messiah the Prince?

_____ weeks + _____ weeks = _____ weeks

Wow! You know that from the time of the issuing of the decree to rebuild Jerusalem until Messiah the prince is 69 weeks! Remember what we learned last week on page 87, about how long these weeks are? We saw that to find out how many years these weeks would be, we had to multiply the weeks by seven.

Turn to your timeline on page 117. We filled in two answers for you, so you could see how to do it. We put the numbers for the weeks from your first blank in the equation above and multiplied it by 7: so 7 weeks x 7 = 49 years, so we put "7 weeks" on one blank and "49 years" on the other blank in the first section.

Now you do the next one. We already did 7 weeks. HOW many weeks did you put in the second blank of the equation above? _____ weeks. Now take that number and multiply it by 7: _____ weeks x 7 = _____ years.

Put these numbers on the correct blanks next to the ones we did. Now look at the top left blanks, and put the total number of weeks added together: 7 weeks + 62 weeks = _____ weeks.

Then take 69 weeks x 7 = _____ years and put the total number of years next to the 69 weeks.

Great! You are a math whiz! When Jesus rode into Jerusalem on a donkey, He was hailed as a prince or a king. This is Jesus coming as Messiah the Prince. This prophecy in Daniel 9:25 shows us the first coming of Jesus Christ, and WHEN it will happen. Sixty-nine weeks (or 483 years) from 445 BC Isn't that cool? HOW are you doing so far? Hang in there! You are going to see some very cool stuff.

Now turn to page 181 and read Daniel 9:25-27.

Daniel 9:26 WHAT does it say about the Messiah?

_____

Let's find out WHAT that means. Look up and read Matthew 27:33-37,45-53.

Matthew 27:35 WHAT did they do to Jesus?

_____

Did you know that when Gabriel told Daniel that the Messiah will be cut off and have nothing, he was giving Daniel a prophecy of Jesus' crucifixion? Jesus died sometime around AD 29. Turn to your timeline and, after "Messiah the Prince comes," draw a cross on your timeline on page 117 to show "Messiah the Prince" is cut off. Remember, this happens around AD 29.
Look back at Daniel 9:26.

Daniel 9:26 WHAT will the *people* of the "prince who is to come" do?

_____

Look up and read Luke 21:20-24.

Luke 21:20 WHAT do you see about Jerusalem?

_____

Luke 21:24 WHAT will happen to Jerusalem?

_____

For HOW long?

_____

Did you know that Jerusalem and the temple were destroyed in AD 70 by Titus, a Roman general? Turn to your timeline on page 117 and write the year the temple was destroyed on your timeline. Then, take a colored pencil and make a mark like this: through the temple to show that it has been destroyed.

Do you realize how incredible this prophecy is that God gave Daniel? God gave the prophecy to Daniel way back in 539 BC, but this prophecy wasn't fulfilled until Jesus came to earth, died on a cross, and the temple was destroyed. Isn't it awesome how God laid out exactly when Jesus would come as Messiah in the Book of Daniel so that His people would know Messiah when He came?

Did they recognize Jesus as the Messiah? No, they didn't. If only they had looked at the details in God's Word, they would have known. That's why we are so proud of you. You are looking at the details so you can know what God's Word says.

Now there are 69 weeks (or 483 years) from the issuing of the decree to rebuild the temple and the first coming of Jesus Christ. And we know that there are 70 weeks decreed for Daniel's people (Daniel 9:24). HOW many weeks are left?

70 weeks - 69 weeks = _____ week or _____ years

Wow! You have just discovered that there is only one week (or seven years) left to fulfill the prophecy that God gave Daniel before Jesus comes back a second time to set up His kingdom on earth.

Remember, the clock started ticking when King Artaxerxes issued a decree to rebuild Jerusalem in 445 BC. Sixty-nine weeks of this prophecy have already taken place. HOW can there only be one week, seven years left? Could there be a time gap between the sixty-ninth and seventieth week? WHERE does it go on our timeline? Hang in there! You'll find out.

Before you leave the set today, solve your new memory verse. Look at the message for Daniel below. Become the script person to help the man dressed in linen get his lines just right in this upcoming episode. Look at the words inside the clouds. As the script person, you need to place each word where it needs to go on the cue card underneath.

Then look up Daniel 10 and find the reference for this verse.

Don't forget: You need to learn these lines and practice them three times in a row, three times every day!

"Now I have _____ to _____ you an
            1   2

_____ of what _____ _____
       3   4   5

to _____ _____ in the _____
    6   7   8

_____ , for the _____ pertains to the
  9   10

_____ _____ _____."
  11   12   13

Daniel 10: ____

Fantastic!

BEHIND THE SCENES

Wasn't it incredible to see how God revealed His plan for the future to Daniel? You saw God give Daniel a 70-week prophecy and discovered that 69 weeks of that prophecy have already happened. Are you ready to find where this last week fits on our timeline? Don't forget to ask God for His help.

HOW many weeks did we discover were left yesterday?

_____ week or _____ years

Let's find out WHERE this week goes on our timeline. Yesterday you looked up Luke 21:24 to find out HOW long Jerusalem would be trampled underfoot by the Gentiles. Pull out your Bible and read this passage again.

HOW long will Jerusalem be trampled underfoot by the Gentiles?

Until the _____ of the _____ are _____

WHAT are the times of the Gentiles? Look at Miss Anna's research in the box below.

PRODUCTION MANAGER'S NOTES

THE TIMES OF THE GENTILES

When Jesus came to earth the first time as Messiah, the Jews did not accept Him as Messiah. Isaiah 53:8 tells us that Jesus will be cut off for the transgressions of His people.

In Luke 19:41-44, Jesus wept because they did not recognize that He was their Messiah (the hour of their visitation). Jesus was cut off. He was crucified. This is when the times of the Gentiles begins.

The times of the Gentiles is the time in history when God is dealing with the Gentile nations, bringing some Gentiles to salvation. When the very last Gentiles who are going to believe in Jesus and accept Him as Savior are saved, then that will be the fullness of the Gentiles.

Some people believe that God has forgotten the Jewish people and that salvation is only for the Gentiles. That is not true! God made an everlasting covenant with the Jewish people. They are His chosen people. Salvation is for both the Jews and the Gentiles. In Romans 11:23-24 we see that we are grafted in with the Jews. In Romans 11:25-26 we see that Israel will be saved when the fullness of the Gentiles has come in.

The messages in Daniel 8–12 are for the Jews. God is showing His people what is going to happen. At the end of the four Gentile kingdoms and the fullness of the Gentiles, God will bring the remnant of Israel (those Jews who believe in Jesus) to salvation with the second coming of Jesus to set up His kingdom on earth. Isn't that exciting?

WHERE would the times of the Gentiles go on the timeline? Did you know that there is an interruption in time in the 70 weeks? From the time Messiah is cut off until the last Gentile is saved there is a break, a time gap in the 70 weeks.

Turn to page 117 and write "Times of the Gentiles" in the blanks over the middle section of your timeline.

Did you know that you are living in the times of the Gentiles? God will not start the last week, the last seven years, until the fullness of the Gentiles. Once the last (Gentile) person gets saved, God's time clock will start again. Could that last one be you?

What can we learn about this last week in Daniel's prophecy? Turn to page 181. Read Daniel 9:25-27.

> Daniel 9:27 WHAT will the prince who is to come make for one week?
>
> _____
>
> HOW long is this week? _____ years
>
> WHAT will he do in the middle of the week?
>
> _____
>
> Since sacrifices are being made, there has to be a temple. Is there a temple in Jerusalem today? _____
>
> Will there be a temple in the future? Look up and read Revelation 11:1. WHAT are they doing?
>
> They are measuring the _____.

Did you know that the Jews are getting the things ready to put in the temple? The Jews are planning and preparing for the rebuilding of their temple.

WHEN will the prince who is to come put a stop to the sacrifice and grain offering?

In the _____ of the _____

HOW would you divide the middle of the week? WHAT is half of seven years? _____ years

So at the halfway point, three-and-a-half years into our final seven years, we see the prince who is to come stop sacrifices and an abomination will come. Turn to your timeline on page 117. The box after the "Times of the Gentiles" is the last week. Divide your week, write how many years go in each half of the box, then write the total at the top of the box.

Isn't that awesome? You have a picture from 445 BC until the last seven years before God sets up His kingdom on earth! Pretty amazing! Now that we know how these 70 weeks fit on the timeline, tomorrow we will take a closer look at this "prince who is to come" in the last week to find out WHO this horrible prince is. Hang in there and take it one step at a time. Don't forget to practice your memory verse.

DAY THREE

A CLOSE-UP SHOT

"Wow, Max, the last two days have been amazing! We have learned so much about the seventy weeks in Daniel. It kinda blows your mind!" exclaimed Molly.

"I can't get over how God has a perfect timeline, and each thing happens just as He plans it. We don't have to worry or get upset when bad things happen because we can see that God has always been and always will be in control."

Aunt Sherry smiled. "I'm so proud of you, Max. You too, Molly." Sam started licking Aunt Sherry's feet. "Okay, Sam, I see you. I guess you've been pretty good. Okay, okay, quit licking. I'm proud of you, too!" Max and Molly cracked up laughing, and Sam barked and sweetly laid his head down.

Aunt Sherry asked, "Are you guys ready to pull out your scripts and see WHOM we can compare this 'prince who is to come' to? We need to have all the details so we can film this terrible episode of the last seven years before Jesus comes back."

"We're ready. I'll pray," Molly volunteered.

Pull out those scripts. WHO could this "prince who is to

come" be? Remember, when we studied Daniel 7, there was "another horn," the "little horn." Could this prince "who is to come" in Daniel 9 be the "little horn" in Daniel 7? Let's find out.

Read Daniel 7:23-25 printed out below. Underline which *kingdom* this is in purple, and color the word *another* and the pronouns that refer to this horn red.

> *Thus he said: "The fourth beast will be a fourth kingdom on the earth, which will be different from all the other kingdoms and will devour the whole earth and tread it down and crush it. As for the ten horns, out of this kingdom ten kings will arise; and another will arise after them, and he will be different from the previous ones and will subdue three kings. He will speak out against the Most High and wear down the saints of the Highest One, and he will intend to make alterations in times and in law; and they will be given into his hand for a time, times, and half a time."*

WHAT kingdom does the little horn come out of?
The _____ kingdom

Now look at your chart on the little horn on page 45 and list what he will do.

Daniel 7:25 He will speak out _____ the _____

_____ and will wear down the _____ of the

_____ _____. He will intend to make _____

in _____ and in _____. The saints will be

given into his hand for a _____, _____,

and _____ a _____.

Do you remember how long "time, times, and half a time" is? It's 3½ years! The saints (the Jews) will be given into this little horn's hand for 3½ years. That sounds pretty bad!

Now let's compare the little horn to the prince who is to come in Daniel 9. Read Daniel 9:27 on the next page and color in red the references to the prince who is to come (the *he*, and *one who makes desolate*).

And he will make a firm covenant with the many for one week, but in the middle of the week he will put a stop to sacrifice and grain offering; and on the wing of abominations will come one who makes desolate, even until a complete destruction, one that is decreed, is poured out on the one who makes desolate.

Daniel 9:27 HOW long will the prince make a covenant for?

_____

HOW long did we discover this week was in years?
_____ years

WHEN will he put a stop to sacrifice and grain offering?

_____

HOW long is that in years? _____ years

This "prince who is to come" is going to break his covenant after 3½ years and stop the Jews from sacrificing and making offerings. He is going to come against the Jews, God's chosen people, just like the "little horn."

Think about what you just saw. The "little horn" in Daniel 7 comes out of the fourth kingdom (the "D.T." beast), which is the last kingdom before the stone crushes the statue and Jesus comes back to set up His kingdom on earth. The saints will be given into the hands of the little horn for 3½ years (time, times, and half a time).

In Daniel 9 we see the "prince who is to come" is in the last seven years before Jesus returns. He is the one who breaks the covenant in the middle of the week, which is also 3½ years.

Do you remember that when we compared the "little horn" to the beast in Revelation 13, we saw the beast was given authority to act for 42 months (3½ years), and that he makes war with and overcomes the saints (the Jews)? All three of these: the "little horn," the "prince who is to come," and "the beast" come out of the same time frame, and they each cause trouble for the saints (the Jews) during these last 3½ years.

Wow! In the last 3½ years, things are going to get very, very bad! But there will be an end. Let's look at what happens to the "little horn," the "prince who is to come," and the beast in Revelation 13. Read Daniel 7:26 to see WHAT happens to the "little horn."

> *But the court will sit for judgment, and his dominion will be taken away, annihilated and destroyed forever.*

WHAT happens to the "little horn"?

_____

_____

The "little horn's" dominion being taken away means he doesn't rule anymore. All right! He is wiped out and destroyed!

WHAT happens to the "prince who is to come" (the one who makes desolate)? Read Daniel 9:27 printed out below.

> *And on the wing of abominations will come one who makes desolate, even until a complete destruction, one that is decreed, is poured out on the one who makes desolate.*

WHAT happens to the prince who is to come?

A complete d__ __ __ __ __ __ __ __ __ __ is poured out

on the _____ who makes _____.

WHAT happens to the beast in Revelation? Look up Revelation 19:20 to find out.

He was thrown in the l __ __ e of f __ __ e !

All right! We know that at the end of the last seven years the "little horn," the "prince who is to come," who is also called "the beast" in Revelation will be destroyed forever!

WHAT will happen next? Look at Daniel 7:27 written below:

> *Then the sovereignty, the dominion and the greatness of all the kingdoms under the whole heaven will be given to the people of the saints of the Highest One; His kingdom will be an everlasting kingdom, and all the dominions will serve and obey Him.*

God's kingdom will be set up on earth. Yippee! God's kingdom will be an everlasting kingdom. This is just like the stone in Daniel 2 that crushes the statue and sets up God's kingdom. Do you know WHO the stone is? J __ __ __ S !

Now that we know that the "prince who is to come" comes out of the last seven years on earth, which is in the fourth kingdom, we need to find out just WHO this fourth kingdom, our "D.T." beast, is.

Look at Daniel 9:26 printed below and underline the phrase "the people of the prince who is to come will destroy the city and the sanctuary" in blue.

> *Then after the sixty-two weeks the Messiah will be cut off and have nothing, and the people of the prince who is to come will destroy the city and the sanctuary. And its end will come with a flood; even to the end there will be war; desolations are determined.*

So WHERE does this "prince who is to come" from? Look at the word *people* in the verse above. This prince comes from the people who will destroy the city (Jerusalem) and the Jewish temple.

When we were working on our timeline, do you remember how we saw Jerusalem and the temple destroyed? Look at page 95.

WHO did we discover destroyed Jerusalem and the temple in A.D. 70?

Titus, a R __ __ __ n general

WHAT kingdom does this general come from? R __ __ e

Guess what? You have just discovered the name of the fourth and final kingdom! The Bible doesn't come out and name this kingdom in Daniel like it has the other three kingdoms, but we can know WHO this kingdom is by looking at history. History tells us that Rome conquered Greece, our third kingdom, in 63 BC.

Let's name all our kingdoms.
WHAT is the first kingdom? _____
The second kingdom? _____
The third kingdom? _____
And so WHO would be the fourth? _____

Turn to the picture of the statue on page 18 and write the name of this fourth kingdom, the kingdom of Rome, beside the legs of iron.

According to Daniel 7, the fourth kingdom, the "D.T." beast (dreadful and terrifying), is different than the other kingdoms. WHAT makes this kingdom different? Let's look at the statue again. It has two legs and ten toes!

Did you know that Rome was eventually divided into two parts—the eastern and the western—just like the two legs? But so far it has never had ten kings—ten toes, ten horns! Could it be that even though the Roman Empire ended, there is another part of the Roman Empire that is yet to come?

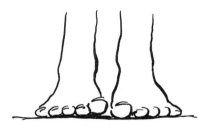

And when it does come, WHAT comes out of the ten horns? Another h __ __ n!

Think about the time gap on our timeline. We are living in the times of the Gentiles. Could the Roman Empire revive after the times of the Gentiles? There seems to be a gap of time on our statue between the legs and the feet. Isn't that incredible? You can look at all the details on the statue at the back of the book on page 167.

God has shown us that there will be ten horns, ten kings, and another one (the little horn) will come out of the ten, but it hasn't happened yet! This part of our statue is yet to come, but God told Daniel about it way back when Nebuchadnezzar was king. Pretty cool, huh?

Even though bad times are coming for Daniel's people and the holy city, there is an end. At the end of the 70 weeks there will be an end to sin, the holy place will be anointed, and Jesus Christ will come again.

God has fast-forwarded us into the future to show us His awesome plan. Always remember: No matter how bad it looks, God is in control. He is judging and putting an end to sin! And in the end, the stone crushes the statue and we win! Amazing!

DAY FOUR

SPECIAL EFFECTS

Today we are going to watch Aunt Sherry shoot a new scene with some amazing special effects as Daniel has another vision.

Just wait until you see this unbelievable man dressed in linen. You aren't going to believe these incredible scenes. But first, don't forget to talk to God.

Grab your script and turn to page 181. Read Daniel 10:1-11 and mark the key words listed in the box below on your Observation Worksheet. Add any new key words to your key-word bookmark.

Key Words for Daniel 10:1-11

Daniel (color it blue)

vision (draw a blue cloud around it)

man dressed in linen (box it in blue and color it yellow)

Don't forget to mark your pronouns! And mark anything that tells you WHERE by double-underlining the WHERE in green. Mark anything that tells you WHEN by drawing a green clock or green circle like this: ○ .

"All right, quiet on the set. We are ready to roll," Aunt Sherry called out. "Camera One, I want you to zoom in on Daniel right after the opening sequence. Let's count it down, and…action."

Daniel 10:1 WHEN is this happening?

_____

Remember, this is the second kingdom, the kingdom of the Medes and the Persians.

WHAT is revealed to Daniel?

_____

WHAT do we see about the message?

_____

This is Daniel's final vision. The last three chapters in Daniel, chapters 10–12, all go together. It is only one vision. Did you know that people put chapter divisions in the Bible in order to make the Bible easier to read, not God?

Daniel 10:2 WHAT has Daniel been doing?

_____

For HOW long? _____

Daniel 10:3 WHAT didn't Daniel do?

_____

Daniel 10:4 WHERE is Daniel?

_____

Daniel 10:5 WHOM does Daniel see?

_____

Daniel 10:5-6 Describe this man.

_____

_____

_____

Isn't this man in linen awesome? Wait until Miss Lenyer adds the special effects. Help her out by drawing a picture of the man dressed in linen in the box.

Daniel 10:7 HOW did the men react, even though they didn't see the vision?

_____

Daniel 10:8 HOW did the vision affect Daniel?

_____

"Mr. Jackson, we need some more powder for Daniel's face," called Aunt Sherry.

Daniel 10:9 WHAT did Daniel do when he heard these words?

_____

Daniel 10:10 HOW does Daniel respond to the man's hand touching him?

_____

Daniel 10:11 HOW does he refer to Daniel?

_____

Daniel has spent his life serving God, and once again we see that he is highly esteemed. He is precious to God.

Daniel 10:11 WHY is this one, this angelic being, here?

_____

WHAT has this angelic being been sent to tell Daniel? We'll find out as we finish this awesome scene tomorrow. Don't forget to practice your memory verse.

DAY FivE

LiGHTS, CAMERA, ACTiON

"Wow, Aunt Sherry, those special effects are so cool!" Molly exclaimed as she, Max, and Aunt Sherry finished watching the first scene with the man dressed in linen.

"How did Miss Lenyer do that?" Max asked. "How did she get him to look like lightning, with those eyes like flaming torches?"

"It's pretty amazing the special effects you can create with computers," replied Aunt Sherry. "But just think: When Daniel saw this man dressed in linen, he saw the real thing. No wonder his knees were shaking together. Are you ready to head back to the set and mark those scripts so we can finish today's scene? Just wait until you see Michael and the prince of the kingdom of Persia!"

"We can't wait," Max replied. "Let's go, Molly."

Don't forget to talk to God. Turn to page 182. Read Daniel 10:12-21 and mark the key words for these verses on your Observation Worksheet. Add any new key words to your bookmark.

Key Words for Daniel 10:12-21

Daniel (color it blue)

vision (draw a blue cloud around it)

man dressed in linen (box it in blue and color it yellow)

God (Lord) (draw a purple triangle and color it yellow)

prince of the kingdom of Persia (circle it in red)

Michael (color it yellow)

latter days (circle it in green and color it red)

Don't forget to mark your pronouns! And mark anything that tells you WHEN by drawing a green clock or green circle like this: ⚪ .

"Great work! Quiet on the set. Camera One, pick up on Daniel. Camera Two, get the man in linen. Stand by…action."

Daniel 10:12 WHAT does he say to Daniel?

"Do _____ be _____."

WHEN was he sent to Daniel?

_____

Isn't that awesome? This angelic being was sent to Daniel the first day Daniel began praying and humbling himself before God. Look back at verse 2.

HOW long had Daniel been mourning?

_____ weeks

Daniel 10:13 WHAT kept the angelic being from coming to Daniel? _____

Now that's interesting. Do you know WHO this prince of the kingdom of Persia is? This is a fallen angel that serves Satan.

HOW long did this fallen angel keep the good angel from coming to Daniel? _____ days

Daniel 10:13 WHO was sent to help this good angel?

_____

WHO is Michael? Let's find out. Look up the passages of Scripture below.

Daniel 10:13 One of the _____ _____

Daniel 10:21 Michael _____ _____

Daniel 12:1 Michael, the _____ _____

Jude 9 Michael the _____

Did you notice the verse that says "Michael your prince," referring to Daniel? Michael is the archangel who stands guard over God's chosen people, the Jews. This is the first time we see Michael involved in a war, but there's another war in heaven in Revelation 12:7, a war between Michael and the dragon (Satan).

WHAT is going on? This is a battle in the heavenly places. The good angel is on his way to bring Daniel an answer to his prayer, when he is stopped by one of the fallen angels of

Satan. Michael has to step in and help in this battle so the angel can get his message to Daniel.

> Daniel 10:14 WHAT is this angel going to give Daniel an understanding of?

> _____

> Daniel 10:16 WHAT came upon Daniel because of this vision?

> _____

> Daniel 10:18 WHAT did the one with human appearance do for Daniel?

> _____

> Daniel 10:19 WHAT did he say to Daniel?

> _____

> _____

> Daniel 10:20 WHAT is he returning to do?

> _____

> Daniel 10:21 WHO is going to stand with him against these forces?

> _____

Wow! What an awesome chapter! Can you imagine having this angelic being appear to you? Did you notice how Daniel kept praying, even when there was no answer? Do you keep praying when you don't get an answer right away? _____

This scene shows us how important our prayers are, and how we need to keep praying and not give up. God hears and answers our prayers! It took 21 days for this heavenly being to get to Daniel.

There is a war in the heavenly places that affects what happens here on earth. Did you know that our battle in this world is against the spiritual forces of wickedness in the heavenly places (Ephesians 6:11-12)? The only way we can protect ourselves is to put on our armor every day, so that we can stand firm against the devil's schemes, his attempts to cause us to fall and sin. HOW do we put on our armor? Look up and read Ephesians 6:13-18.

Draw a picture of you in the box below.

Now add each piece of armor as you read about it. Then write the name of each piece beside it on your drawing. This will help you learn and remember each piece.

1. Draw the first piece, the belt of t __ __ __ __ .

   How can you put on this belt every day? By studying and memorizing God's Word.

2. Draw the _____ of _____.

   The breastplate protected a soldier's vital organs, like his heart, lungs, stomach, and kidneys, so the enemy's arrows could not get through and kill him. HOW can you protect yourself? By doing what God says is right and staying away from sin. Then the enemy can't touch you!

3. Draw some sandals on your feet to represent putting the _____ of _____ on your feet.

In Roman times, the sandals had "grippers" so they could stand firm and not slip and slide. When you know that you belong to God by accepting Jesus Christ in your life, then there is a peace in your heart. You can stand firm because you are on God's side and He's on yours, and the devil can't win against God!

4. Draw the _____ of _____.

This shield let the soldier put out the flaming arrows that were shot at him. The next time the enemy throws a lie or a doubt or an accusation at you, put up that shield. Remind the devil what God's Word says. Give him a verse that shows he is wrong. For example, when he says, "You're not good enough," then you can say, "You're wrong! I am good enough. I am chosen by God to go and bear fruit" (John 15:16). Remember, when Jesus was tempted by the devil in the wilderness, He handled every temptation by quoting God's Word. The more you know God's Word, the stronger your shield will be.

5. Draw the _____ of _____.

To protect your mind, you need to remember to whom you belong. Christ lives inside Christians, and He is stronger than the enemy. First John 4:4 tells you that Jesus who is in you is greater than the devil (and his cohorts), who is in the world. Keep your helmet on!

6. Draw the _____ of the _____.

The sword of the Spirit is God's Word. It's your one and only offensive weapon because it is all you need for victory. The only way you can fight is with God's Word. Pull that sword out of its sheath and use it!

And don't forget to pray at all times.

All right! Now practice putting on your armor each and every day so that you can stand firm and resist the devil! Outstanding! Keep up the good work, valiant warrior!

TIME GAP

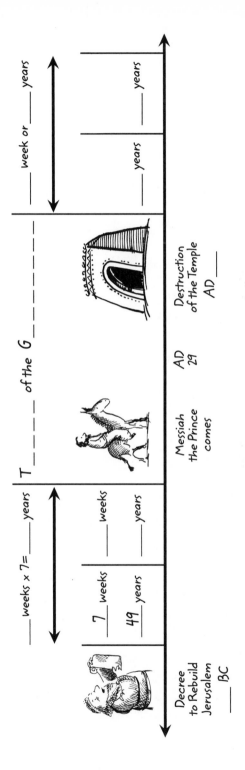

____ week or ____ years

____ weeks x 7 = ____ years

T _ _ _ _ _ of the G _ _ _ _ _ _ _

7 weeks	
49 years	____ weeks
	____ years

____ years

____ years

Decree
to Rebuild
Jerusalem
____ BC

Messiah
the Prince
comes

AD
29

Destruction
of the Temple
AD ____

6

THE BATTLE OF THE KINGS

DANIEL 11

Are you ready to start another amazing week on the set? Last week we not only discovered when the 70-week prophecy began, but we also saw that there is only one week left before Jesus comes back to set up His kingdom on earth. Isn't that exciting?

We saw that the "little horn" of Daniel 7, the "prince who is to come" of Daniel 9, and the beast of Revelation 13 are all the same person—a horrible king that comes out of the fourth kingdom in those last seven years. And we even saw that the fourth kingdom, that of the "D.T." beast, is the kingdom of Rome.

Incredible, but it isn't over yet. When we left Daniel, he was having another vision where he saw a man dressed in linen. Let's find out WHAT happens next. Let's head out on location to discover more about Daniel's last vision.

DAY ONE

LIGHTS, CAMERA, ACTION...

"Whoa, Aunt Sherry!" Max exclaimed as he and Molly arrived on location. "Those are some awesome horses and costumes. This is going to be so cool." Sam jumped out of Max's arms and started running toward the soldiers and barking like crazy. "Sam, Sam! Come back here. Come on, Molly, we better go catch him before he upsets the horses."

Now that Max and Molly have captured "you know who," we can start filming this very cool episode. This is a very hard chapter, but what makes it so amazing is that in this chapter God is showing Daniel in detail what is going to happen before it ever happens. In Daniel 11–12, God is going to take Daniel and show him what happens from the times of the Medes and the Persians (the second kingdom) all the way through the end of time. Can you believe that?

Because it is so detailed, we are just going to get the big picture. Hang in there and don't give up! Miss Kay and Miss Janna are so very proud of you!

All right! Don't forget to pray. You need to talk to God big time about Daniel 11! Quiet on the set. Lights, camera, and action.

Turn to page 183. Read Daniel 11:1-4.

Daniel 11:1 WHEN is this happening?

_____

WHAT kingdom is ruling? _____

WHO is this who rose to be an encouragement to Daniel? Look back at Daniel 10:21. WHO was speaking?

_____

Daniel 11:2 WHAT does the heavenly being tell Daniel?

_____ kings will arise in _____.

Let's name these three kings who are going to arise in Persia. Look at the chart "The Rulers and Prophets of Daniel's Time" below for the names of the Persian kings who ruled after Darius the Mede. (Don't count Smerdis. He only reigned for a short time—maybe only a few days.)

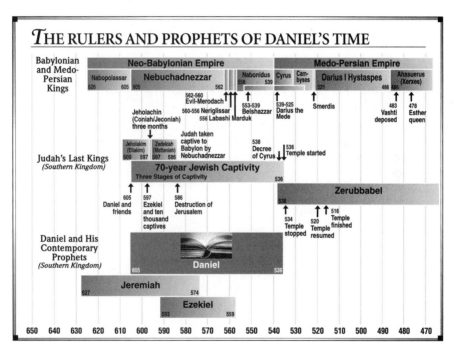

Name the first three kings of Persia (except Smerdis).

1. C __ __ __ s

2. C__ __ __ __ __ __ s

3. D __ __ __ __ __   I H__ __ __ __ __ __ __ s

WHO is the fourth king? (Look at your chart)

4. A _ _ _ _ _ _ _ s (X_ _ _ _ s)

Did you know that the name of this fourth king is the same name as King Artaxerxes? Artaxerxes (or Ahasuerus, or Xerxes) is the king we read about in Nehemiah 2 who issued a decree for Nehemiah to rebuild the wall and the city of Jerusalem.

Daniel 11:2 WHAT does the fourth king do?

The fourth will gain far more _____ and he will arouse the whole _____ against _____.

Think about what we learned in Daniel 8. Remember the ram (who represented the kingdom of the Medes and Persians) going up against the goat (the kingdom of Greece)?

Daniel 11:3 WHAT do we see about this king?

_____

Daniel 11:4 WHAT do we see about his kingdom?

His kingdom will be _____ up and _____

out toward the _____ points of the compass, though

not to his own _____. His sovereignty will be

_____ and _____ to _____ besides them.

WHO is the king with the kingdom that is broken up and parceled out to four points of the compass? Does this description of a broken kingdom and four points of the compass remind you of something you have heard before?

HOW about a goat with a broken horn and four horns that come up in its place? HOW about that very fast leopard with four heads?

WHAT kingdom is this?

_____

Do you remember WHO the first king of Greece was? We read about him on pages 63-64. Write his name if you remember. _____

    The king in Daniel 11:3-4 is Alexander the Great. Remember, he didn't have an appointed heir, so four of his generals divided his kingdom. Someday when you study Greek history, you're going to see this and you will already know all about it!

    Take a look at the chart below, "History of Israel's Relationship to the Kings of Daniel 11."

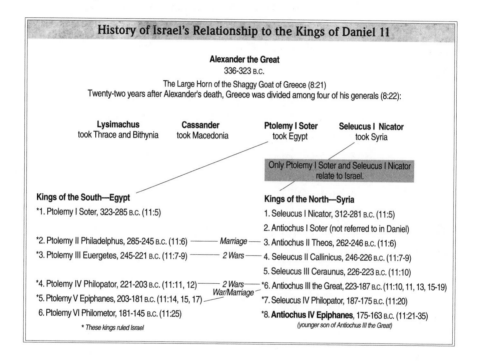

History of Israel's Relationship to the Kings of Daniel 11

Alexander the Great
336-323 B.C.

The Large Horn of the Shaggy Goat of Greece (8:21)
Twenty-two years after Alexander's death, Greece was divided among four of his generals (8:22):

Lysimachus	**Cassander**	**Ptolemy I Soter**	**Seleucus I Nicator**
took Thrace and Bithynia	took Macedonia	took Egypt	took Syria

Only Ptolemy I Soter and Seleucus I Nicator relate to Israel.

Kings of the South—Egypt

*1. Ptolemy I Soter, 323-285 B.C. (11:5)

*2. Ptolemy II Philadelphus, 285-245 B.C. (11:6) —— Marriage ——

*3. Ptolemy III Euergetes, 245-221 B.C. (11:7-9) —— 2 Wars ——

*4. Ptolemy IV Philopator, 221-203 B.C. (11:11, 12) —— 2 Wars ——
War/Marriage
*5. Ptolemy V Epiphanes, 203-181 B.C. (11:14, 15, 17)

6. Ptolemy VI Philometor, 181-145 B.C. (11:25)

          * These kings ruled Israel

Kings of the North—Syria

1. Seleucus I Nicator, 312-281 B.C. (11:5)

2. Antiochus I Soter (not referred to in Daniel)

3. Antiochus II Theos, 262-246 B.C. (11:6)

4. Seleucus II Callinicus, 246-226 B.C. (11:7-9)

5. Seleucus III Ceraunus, 226-223 B.C. (11:10)

*6. Antiochus III the Great, 223-187 B.C. (11:10, 11, 13, 15-19)

*7. Seleucus IV Philopator, 187-175 B.C. (11:20)

*8. **Antiochus IV Epiphanes**, 175-163 B.C. (11:21-35)
         (younger son of Antiochus III the Great)

    The book of Daniel is only concerned with the last two generals of Alexander the Great because they and their descendants ruled over Israel at different times. Remember, the prophecy in Daniel is about what's going to happen to God's chosen people, the nation of Israel.

    Look at the last two generals on the chart.

    WHAT general took Egypt? _____

His descendants are the kings of the S __ __ __ h

WHAT general took Syria? _____

His descendants are the kings of the N __ __ __ h

WHY are these kings called the kings of the North and the kings of the South? Israel is the Beautiful Land. Many people refer to it as Palestine, but the Bible never calls it Palestine. Israel is the land that God promised to Abraham, Isaac, and Jacob (Israel) as an everlasting possession. So WHERE is Israel located geographically? It's between the two lands of Egypt and Syria. Egypt is south of Israel, which is why they are called the kings of the South. Syria is north of Israel, which is why they are called the kings of the North.

WHAT will Daniel's vision show us about these kings of the North and kings of the South? We'll find out as we continue filming this episode. You have done an awesome job today!

Show Ryan, our art director, how smart you are. He has created a rebus just for you to uncover your memory verse.

A rebus is a word puzzle that mixes pictures and words. When you combine the pictures and the letters by adding or subtracting letters, you will end up with a new word. Solve the rebus and write out your answer on the lines on the next page. Don't forget to look for your reference.

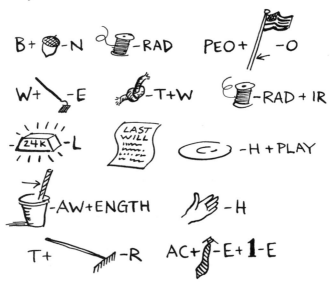

Daniel 11: _____

You did it! Now practice saying this verse three times today!

DAY TWO

ON LOCATION

"Max, why don't you and Molly come over here and give me a hand?" called out Mr. Leon, the animal trainer.

"Sure thing, Mr. Leon," Max replied. "We had so much fun helping with the horses yesterday."

Molly winked at Mr. Leon. "Sam was really helpful, wasn't he?"

Mr. Leon smiled. "Sam, show Max and Molly what you learned this morning after I caught you in the stable." Mr. Leon gave the signal, and Sam started galloping like a horse, throwing back his head. "Good boy. Here's your treat."

"Wow, Mr. Leon, maybe I need to take lessons from you," exclaimed Max. Everyone burst out laughing. Mr. Leon wiped tears out of his eyes as he tried to quit laughing. "Okay, we'd better get these horses to your Aunt Sherry. She should be ready to film them anytime now."

The horses are ready to go. Don't forget to ask God for His help.

Then turn to page 184. Read Daniel 11:5-10 and mark the key words from the box below. Add any new key words to your keyword bookmark.

Key Words for Daniel 11:5-10

king of the South (underline it in green)

king of the North (underline it in orange)

Don't forget to mark your pronouns! And mark anything that tells you WHERE by double-underlining the <u>WHERE</u> in green. Mark anything that tells you WHEN by drawing a green clock ⏰ or green circle like this: ◯ .

"Okay, places everyone," Aunt Sherry called out. "Mr. Leon, are the kings and the horses ready? Quiet on the set. Stand by. And action."

To help you see WHAT kings ruled WHEN in Daniel 11:5-10, look at your chart "History of Israel's Relationship to the Kings of Daniel 11" on page 123.

WHO is the first king of the South?

_____

Turn to page 184. Write this king's name beside Daniel 11:5. (Use a green pen or pencil since we underlined the kings of the South in green.)

Look at your chart. WHO is the next king of the South in Daniel 11:6?

_____

Write his name next to Daniel 11:6 on your Observation Worksheet.

On your chart, WHO is the next king of the South in Daniel 11:7-9?

_____

Write his name next to Daniel 11:7-9.

Great! Now let's look at the kings of the North on the chart for Daniel 11:5-10.

WHO is the first king of the North in Daniel 11:5?

_____

Write this king's name beside Daniel 11:5 in orange since we underlined the kings of the North in orange.

Looking at your chart, WHO is the king of the North in Daniel 11:6?

_____

Write this king's name in orange next to Daniel 11:6.

WHO is the king of the North in Daniel 11:7-9?

_____

Write this king's name in orange next to Daniel 11:7-9.

WHO is the king of the North in Daniel 11:10?

_____

Write his name in orange next to Daniel 11:10.

Way to go! Did writing the kings' names on your Observation Worksheet help you keep up with all these different kings and their conflicts? Don't get discouraged. This is a hard passage for grown-ups, too! Tomorrow we will continue looking at these kings.

DAY THREE

SEND IN THE KINGS

"Are the kings ready?" Aunt Sherry radioed Olivia.

"They sure are. Mr. Jackson is putting the final touches on their makeup, and then they will be right out."

"Great!" Aunt Sherry answered. "Okay, Grayson, we are about ready to go. The kings are on their way. Are the horses ready, Mr. Leon?"

"Yes, ma'am. We're ready to ride."

Aunt Sherry smiled at Mr. Leon. "Then, places everybody. Quiet on the set. We're ready to roll."

How about you? Are you ready to continue looking at these awesome kings that God showed Daniel in his vision? Don't forget to talk to God! Then turn to page 184. Read Daniel 11:11-20 and mark the key words in the box below for these verses.

Key Words for Daniel 11:11-20

king of the South (underline it in green)

king of the North (underline it in orange)

vision (draw a blue cloud around it)

the Beautiful Land (double-underline it in green and color it blue)

Don't forget to mark your pronouns! And mark anything that tells you WHEN by drawing a green clock 🕐 or green circle like this: ○ .

Now let's discover WHO these kings are in Daniel 11:11-20. Turn to your chart, the "History of Israel's Relationship to the Kings of Daniel 11" on page 123. Look at the king of the South on your chart for Daniel 11:11.

WHO is the king of the South in Daniel 11:11-12?

_____

Turn to page 184. Write this king's name beside Daniel 11:11. (Use a green pen or pencil since we underlined the kings of the South in green.)

WHO is the next king of the South in Daniel 11:14, 15,17?

_____

Write his name next to Daniel 11:14 on your Observation Worksheet and write "Daniel 11:14,15,17" under his name.

All right! Now let's look at the kings of the North in Daniel 11:11-20.

> WHO is the king of the North in Daniel 11:10,11,13,15-19?

> _____

Write the king of the North's name beside Daniel 11:10, 11,13,15,19 in orange since we underlined the kings of the North in orange.

> WHO is the king of the North in Daniel 11:20?

> _____

Write this king's name beside Daniel 11:20 in orange.

Fantastic! We are so proud of your patience as you looked at each one of these kings. It gets confusing, but it is very important! Don't forget to practice your memory verse! Tomorrow we are going to zoom in on one of the kings of the North.

DAY FOUR

ZOOMING IN

That was a fantastic scene you shot yesterday of the kings of the South and the kings of the North and their conflicts. Whew! Keeping up with all those kings took a lot of hard work, but you did it! Today we are going to zoom in and get a close-up of one of the kings of the North. Don't forget to pray.

Turn to page 185. Read Daniel 11:21-24 and mark the pronouns or words in these verses that refer to the *king of the North* that arises by underlining them in orange on your Observation

Worksheet. And mark anything that tells you WHEN by drawing a green clock 🕐 or green circle like this: ⃝ .

Remember, all we're doing is getting the big picture. This is very hard for grown-ups, too! How cool that you are doing it on your own!

Do you remember WHO the small horn was in Daniel 8:9-12 who came out of the kingdom of Greece? Remember, he was a very horrible king. WHO did we discover the small horn is? You can do a sneak peek back at page 70 if you aren't sure.

This is the king of the North in Daniel 11:21-35. Turn to page 185 and write the king's name, Antiochus IV Epiphanes, in orange beside Daniel 11:21, and under his name write "Daniel 11:21-35." We've heard about this king and the things he's done before. Now we see him again in Daniel 11. Let's see WHAT else we can learn about this horrible king.

Daniel 11:21 HOW is he described?

_____

HOW did he get the kingdom?

_____

Daniel 11:23 WHAT is made with him?

_____

WHAT will he practice?

_____

HOW will he gain power?

_____

Daniel 11:24 WHAT will he do?

_____

_____

Is there an end to what he will do? _____

Wow! This king is called a despicable person. He comes on the scene to seize the kingdom by intrigue. WHAT else does this king do? We'll find out tomorrow as we continue looking at this king of the North, Antiochus IV Epiphanes. Don't forget to practice your memory verse!

DAY FIVE

A CLOSE-UP OF THE KING

All right! Quiet on the set. Is Antiochus IV ready to ride? Today as we film this awesome scene, we're going to look at this king of the North and the last king of the South. Don't forget to ask God for His help. Then turn to page 186. Read Daniel 11:25-35 and mark the key words from the box below for these verses. Add any new key words to your key-word bookmark.

Key Words for Daniel 11:25-35

king of the North (underline it in orange)

king of the South (underline it in green)

holy covenant (covenant) (box it in yellow and color it red)

sanctuary fortress (color it blue)

---

the regular sacrifice (color it pink)

abomination of desolation (color it red)

the end time (circle it in green and color it red)

God (draw a purple triangle and color it yellow)

Don't forget to mark your pronouns! And mark anything that tells you WHEN by drawing a green clock ⏰ or green circle like this: ◯ .

Now get a close-up. WHO is this king of the South? Look at your chart on page 123 and write his name in green next to Daniel 11:25.

Daniel 11:25 WHAT will the king of the South do?

_____

Will he stand? _____ WHY or WHY not? _____

_____

Daniel 11:27 WHAT are both kings' hearts intent on?

_____

WHAT will they speak to each other? _____

WHY won't it succeed?

_____

Daniel 11:28 WHOM is the heart of the king of the North, Antiochus IV Epiphanes, set against?

_____

Daniel 11:30 WHO comes against him?

_____

WHAT will he do when he is disheartened?

_____

HOW will he treat those who forsake the holy covenant?

_____

Daniel 11:31 WHAT will forces from him do?

_____

_____

_____

We have seen this before, haven't we, in Daniel 8:11-14? Do you remember reading about Antiochus IV Epiphanes doing this on page 70?

Daniel 11:32 WHAT did we see about those who know their God?

_____

Daniel 11:33 WHAT will happen to those who have insight?

"They will give _____ to the many; yet they

will _____ by the _____ and

by _____, by _____ and by _____

for _____ _____."

Daniel 11:35 WHAT will happen to some of the ones who have insight?

_____

_____

WHEN does the end time come?

At the _____ _____

Isn't this amazing? The end has an appointed time. God is in control of time and events! When Daniel received this vision, it was 536 BC. This king of the North, the small horn in Daniel 8, Antiochus IV Epiphanes, didn't come on the scene until 175 BC. Just look at the details we see in Daniel's vision. Think about the horrible things Antiochus IV Epiphanes did. Remember how he put up a statue of Zeus, stopped sacrifices, and sacrificed a pig on the altar? HOW incredible that God would show Daniel exactly what would happen in the future. No wonder Daniel was in anguish. Even though he would not be here, he saw the horrors that would happen to his people.

Is the end time the same time of "A.E." (Antiochus IV Epiphanes), or is this end time still to come? That's what we are going to look at next week. Let's think about "A.E." Could it be that Antiochus IV Epiphanes is giving us a picture of someone who is to come at the end time? WHO could that be?

Don't forget to practice your memory verse! Say it out loud to a grown-up to remind you that those who know their God will display strength and take action. Way to go! We are so very proud of you!

7

A TIME OF DISTRESS

DANIEL 11-12

Can you believe that this is the last week of filming our television series? It has been such an incredible adventure! WHAT did you think about all those kings last week as we got the big picture of the kings of the North and the kings of the South from the time of the Medes and Persians until the very end of time? Were you surprised to discover that Antiochus IV Epiphanes, the small horn in Daniel 8, was also the king of the North in Daniel 11:21-35?

Is this king of the North, Antiochus IV Epiphanes, giving us a picture of someone who is to come at the end time? Let's find out. Head back to our awesome location as we shine the spotlight on the last king in Daniel 11.

DAY ONE

SPOTLIGHT ON A KING

"Okay, guys, we're about ready to roll," Aunt Sherry called out as she walked toward the cameraman. "Grayson, I want some close-ups of this king. I want to make sure our viewers catch the expression on his face as he comes on the scene. Max, will you and Molly check with Miss Olivia and make sure our king is ready?"

"Here he comes now, Aunt Sherry," Max called out, as the king walked out of his dressing room.

"Places, everybody. We're ready to roll. Play back music. Stand by and action."

Are you ready to take a close-up look at this king? Grab your scripts. Turn to page 187. Read Daniel 11:36-45 and mark the key words listed below on your Observation Worksheet. Add any new key words to your bookmark.

Key Words for Daniel 11:36-45

the king (color it red)

God (draw a purple triangle and color it yellow)

the end time (circle it in green and color it red)

king of the South (underline it in green)

king of the North (underline it in orange)

the Beautiful Land (double-underline it in green and color it blue)

Don't forget to mark your pronouns! And mark anything that tells you WHERE by double-underlining the WHERE in green.

Mark anything that tells you WHEN by drawing a green clock 🕐 or green circle like this: ◯ .
Now let's make a list about this king.

The King in Daniel 11:36-45

Daniel 11:36 He will do as he _____. He will

_____and _____ himself above every

_____ and will speak _____ things against

the_____ of _____. He will _____until

the _____ is _____.

Daniel 11:37 He will show no regard for the _____

of his fathers or the desire of _____, or show

regard for any other _____. He will _____

himself _____ them all.

Daniel 11:38 He will honor a _____ of _____.

He will honor him with _____, _____, costly

_____ and _____.

Daniel 11:39 He will take _____ against the

_____ of _____ with the help of a foreign

_____. He will give great _____ to those

who _____ him and will cause them to _____

over the _____. He will parcel out _____

for a _____.

Daniel 11:40 He will collide with the _____ of

the _____, and the _____ of the _____

will _____ against him.

He will enter _____, _____ them and _____ through.

Daniel 11:41 He will enter the _____ _____, and many _____ will _____.

Daniel 11:43 He will gain _____ over the hidden _____ of _____ and _____ and over all the _____ things of _____. The _____ and _____ will follow at his _____.

Daniel 11:44 He will go forth with great _____ to _____ and _____ many.

Daniel 11:45 He will pitch the _____ of his _____ _____ between the _____ and the beautiful _____ _____. He will come to his _____ and _____ _____ will _____ him.

Wow! Did you know that this is a prophecy of a king who hasn't come yet? What is so exciting and interesting about all that we are studying about these kings in Daniel 11 is that at this time in history we can look back by studying history and see how the prophecy of every king in Daniel 11:2-35 has been fulfilled.

But all the way back, up until now, we have never seen a king like the king that is described in Daniel 11:36-45. This is a prophecy that hasn't been fulfilled yet! This is a guy we want to watch out for. That's why we made a list and got God's description of him to help us discover his M.O., his method of operation.

Remember how Daniel describes the "small horn" in Daniel 8, and then gives us another description in Daniel 11:21-35? The "small horn" in Daniel 8 is the king in Daniel 11:21-35, who we discovered was Antiochus IV Epiphanes. Could it be that the king in Daniel 11:36-45 is another description of the "little horn" in Daniel 7? This is the king that Antiochus IV Epiphanes gives us a picture of.

Look back at Daniel 11:45 on your chart on page 138.

> WHAT happens to this king?
>
> _____
>
> Now let's make some comparisons. Think about all you have learned in Daniel's visions. WHAT happens to the "little horn" in Daniel 7:26?
>
> _____
>
> _____
>
> HOW about the "prince who is to come" (the one who make desolate) in Daniel 9:27?
>
> _____
>
> WHAT happens to the beast in Revelation 19:20?
>
> _____
>
> Could this king in Daniel 11:36-45 be the "little horn," the "prince who is to come," and "the beast"? _____

Yes! All four of these are a picture of the person who will come on the scene in the last week of Daniel's 70-week prophecy. Does this person have any other names? You'll find out as we continue to film our series!

Now let's discover this week's memory verse. Look at the stars shining brightly in the expanse of heaven. Each star has a word from your memory verse that has been mixed up. Start with the first star and unscramble the letters inside the star and place each letter on the correct blanks underneath the picture. After you have unscrambled each word, take a look at Daniel 12 to find the reference for this verse.

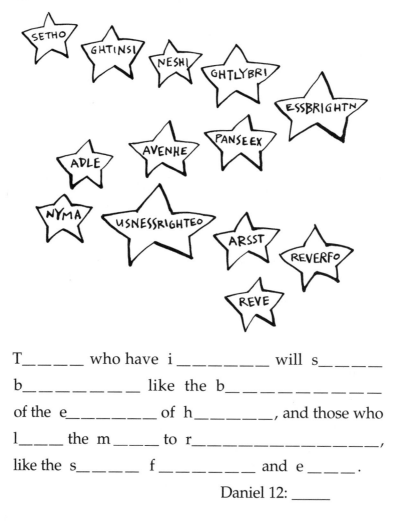

T_____ who have i _____ will s_____

b_____ like the b_____

of the e_____ of h_____, and those who

l_____ the m_____ to r_____,

like the s_____ f_____ and e_____.

Daniel 12:_____

All right! Don't forget to practice this verse three times in a row, three times today!

DAY TWO

TAKE TWO: MICHAEL STANDS GUARD

"Wow, Aunt Sherry!" Molly exclaimed. "That was a very scary scene on the last king in Daniel 11. It's so hard to believe that there will be someone who does such horrible things."

"I know. But even though bad times are coming, always remember that God is in control. He has a perfect plan for the future. We need to trust Him so we can be a light in the darkness, just like the stars that shine brightly in our memory verse."

"That's pretty cool!" Max replied.

Aunt Sherry smiled. "Yes, it is. Now grab your scripts and mark the next scene so we can find out what else happens at the time of this last king. Don't forget to ask God to help you understand."

Are you ready to start shining like the stars? Great! Turn to page 188. Today we are only going to mark one verse, Daniel 12:1. Read this verse and mark the key words from the box below. Add any new key words to your key-word bookmark.

Key Words for Daniel 12:1

Michael (color it yellow)

the sons of your people (your people) (draw a blue star of David)

time of distress (box it in black)

Don't forget to mark anything that tells you WHEN by drawing a green clock or green circle like this: ○ .

Now come in close.

Daniel 12:1 WHEN is this happening? WHAT is the time phrase that is used here?

"Now at _____ _____"

Go back and read Daniel 11:45 through Daniel 12:1.

Daniel 12:1 is a continuation of Daniel 11:45. Remember what we talked about earlier: The Bible wasn't written in chapters and verses. Man is the one who added them later.

WHAT connects Daniel 11:45 to Daniel 12:1? It's the time phrase in Daniel 12:1. Can you find it? Write it out on the blanks below.

"_____ _____ _____ _____"

Up to this point in Daniel, everything has happened just like God said it would. But remember what we saw yesterday? This king hasn't come yet, so this hasn't happened. WHEN does it happen? It happens at the end time.

Daniel 12:1 WHO will arise at this time?

_____

WHO is Michael? And WHAT is his job?

_____

WHAT will this time be like?

_____

WHAT do you learn about this time of distress?

A time of distress such as _____ _____ since

there was a _____ until that _____

As you have studied the Book of Daniel, do you remember seeing other places where Daniel's people would go through hard times? Let's review. Look back at Daniel 7:21 on page 175.

Daniel 7:21 WHOM was the horn waging war with?

_____

Read Daniel 7:25. WHO was given into the little horn's hand for time, times, and half a time?

The _____ of the Highest One

Read Daniel 9:27 on page 181.

WHOM does the prince who is to come make a covenant with?

_____

Look up and read Revelation 13:7. WHOM did the beast make war with?

_____

The *saints* and the *many* in these passages of Scripture are referring to God's chosen people, the Jews, the nation of Israel. From looking at these passages of Scripture, you can see how God's people are going to go through some very hard times when the little horn, the prince who is to come, the beast of Revelation, and the king in Daniel 11:36-45 comes on the scene. Could this be the time of distress in Daniel 12:1? Look back at Daniel 12.

Daniel 12:1 WHO will be rescued?

_____

_____

That's pretty awesome! A time of distress is coming for God's people, but if their names are found written in the book, they will be rescued!

Even in this time of distress, we see Michael, a great prince, standing guard over God's people. God never leaves or forsakes us. He is always there.

Amazing! Don't forget to practice your memory verse.

DAY THREE

BACKGROUND CHECK

Wasn't it exciting to discover Michael, the great prince, standing guard over God's people during the time of distress on earth? Can you even imagine a time worse than anything else that has ever happened in history? WHAT else can we learn about this time at the end? Let's do a background check to see what else the Bible has to say about this time of distress. We need to pull out our scripts and compare Scripture with Scripture! Don't forget to pray!

Now look up and read Joel 2:1-2.

Joel 2:1 WHAT does God tell them to sound?

_____

WHY are all the inhabitants of the land to tremble?

_____

Joel 2:2 WHAT will this day be like?

A day of _____ and _____, a day of

_____ and thick _____. There has _____been

_____ like it, nor will there be _____ after it.

Look up and read Jeremiah 30:6-7.

Jeremiah 30:7 WHAT do we see about that day?

_____

WHAT is that day the time of?

It is the time of _____ _____.

WHAT will happen?

He will be _____ from it.

Look up and read Matthew 24:15-22.

Matthew 24:15 WHAT was standing in the holy place?

The _____ of _____

Matthew 24:16 WHAT are the people who are in Judea
to do?

_____

Matthew 24:17 WHAT are those to do who are on the
housetops?

Do not _____ _____ to get the _____ that are

in his _____.

Matthew 24:18 WHAT is the one in the field to do?

He must _____ _____ _____ to get his _____.

Matthew 24:20 WHAT are they to pray?

That their _____ will not be in _____ or on

a _____

Matthew 24:21 WHAT will there be such as never has occurred since the beginning of the world until now, nor ever will?

A _____ _____

Matthew 24:22 WHAT do we see about the time of "those days"?

They are _____ _____.

WHY were they cut short?

_____

_____

Draw a picture of what you think this time of distress might look like in the box below.

Wow! Think about what you have just learned about this time of distress. This time is going to be so bad that God's people are to flee Jerusalem when they see the Abomination of Desolation standing in the holy place. They are not even to go back to get their cloak.

So WHO is this Abomination of Desolation standing in the holy place? Have we seen anything that sounds like this before? How about when Antiochus IV Epiphanes put up a statue of Zeus inside the temple, stopped sacrifices, and sacrificed a pig on the altar? This Abomination of Desolation desecrates the temple just like Antiochus IV Epiphanes (A.E.) did! Remember, A.E. is showing us a picture of one who is coming. A.E. is a picture of the last king in Daniel 11:36-45. And WHO did we discover this last king is?

The l __ __ __ __ e h __ __ n in Daniel 7,

The p __ __ __ __ e who is to c __ __ e in Daniel 9,

The b __ __ __ t in Revelation 13.

Could this Abomination of Desolation standing in the holy place in Matthew be another name in the Bible for the last king in Daniel 11:36-45?

He fits the time frame. He is standing in the holy place. Could he be magnifying himself to be God like we see the last king in Daniel 11:36 doing? The Jews are to flee, which sounds like he is coming after them, just like we saw the little horn, the prince who is to come, and the beast overcome the saints. Yes, this last king is also the Abomination of Desolation in Matthew 24.

Do you know any other names for this king? Can you think of anyone who will cause a time of distress in the last 3½ years on earth? Write out the name if you think you know WHO this is.

All right! Don't forget to practice your memory verse! Shine like those stars in the expanse.

DAY FOUR

SPECIAL EFFECTS

"Hey, guys, are you ready to film another cool scene with special effects?" Miss Lenyer asked Max and Molly.

"That sounds awesome!" Max replied. "Molly and I are almost finished marking our scripts."

Molly looked up and smiled. "We can't wait to see how you are going to shoot the scene of those sleeping in the ground."

"You'll love it! Why don't you both head over to Set B as soon as you're finished with your scripts? We should be ready to shoot in about fifteen minutes."

"We'll be there!"

How about you? Are you ready? Don't forget to talk to God. Then turn to page 188. Read Daniel 12:1-7 and mark the key words in your script for verses 2-7. Add any new key words to your key-word bookmark.

Key Words for Daniel 12:2-7

those who have insight (color it orange)

Daniel (color it blue)

end of time (circle it in green and color it red)

man dressed in linen (box it in blue and color it yellow)

God (draw a purple triangle and color it yellow)

the holy people (draw a blue star of David)

Don't forget to mark your pronouns! And mark anything that tells you WHEN by drawing a green clock 🕐 or green circle like this: ○ .

"All right! Quiet on the set. Camera One, I want a tight shot."

Daniel 12:2 WHAT will happen to many of those who sleep in the dust of the ground?

_____

WHAT will happen to others?

_____

That means that everyone is not going to heaven. Some people are going into everlasting contempt, to the lake of fire!

Daniel 12:3 WHAT will happen to those with insight?

_____

HOW about those who lead the many to righteousness?

_____

Have you ever noticed how bright the stars look in the dark? Do we shine brighter when we are in the dark, hard times? Do people see you shine when the rest of your friends do mean things like making fun of a kid, saying bad words, or cheating so they can win? _____ Did you know that when you don't go along with the crowd, when you do what God says is right, that's when you shine?

Daniel 12:4 WHAT was Daniel to do?

_____

Until WHEN? The _____ of _____

Wow! Does the fact that we can understand this book now show we are getting close to the end?

Daniel 12:5 WHOM did Daniel see?

_____

Daniel 12:6 WHAT did the one ask the man dressed in linen?

_____

Daniel 12:7 HOW long would it be?

_____

We have seen this time phrase before. HOW long is this?

_____

WHEN will all these events be complete?

As soon as they _____ _____ the _____

of the _____ _____

And WHO are the holy people? WHO are Daniel's people?

_____

Remember when we looked at Daniel 7:21,25; Daniel 9:27; and Revelation 13:7 and saw how the little horn, the prince who is to come, and the beast overcame the saints? *Saints* is another word for holy ones. Daniel 12:7 is showing us the shattering of the power of God's holy people, which are the saints who are God's chosen people, the Jews. But is it forever? No way!

WHAT's our time frame in Daniel 12:7?

_____, _____, and _____ a _____

Which is HOW long in years? _____

Then WHAT happens? Take a peek back at Daniel 7:27 on page 175.

WHAT was given to the people of the saints of the Highest One?

_____

WHAT do we see about God's kingdom?

_____

And don't forget about the statue in Daniel 2:34-35.

WHAT crushes the feet and causes the whole statue to crumble?

The s __ __ __ e

And WHO is this? _____ ____ _____ ____ _____!

All right! You did an awesome job! The power of the holy people will be shattered, but only for 3½ years, and then Jesus will come back, the little horn will be destroyed, and God's kingdom will endure forever!

THE FINAL SCENE

"Okay, guys, this is it," Aunt Sherry called out. "This is the final scene in our television series on Daniel. You have done such a wonderful job."

Molly looked at her Aunt Sherry and made a funny face. "My head is spinning, thinking about all the things we have uncovered in Daniel's visions. Will we ever be able to keep all these beasts, horns, and kings straight?" Max, Aunt Sherry, and Miss Leslie all started laughing.

"It is a lot to remember," Aunt Sherry teased. "That's why God gave you His awesome script, the Bible. We have to study it every day! And that's why we're making this television series, so kids can learn about God's plan for the future. Let's grab our scripts and shoot the ending to this awesome series."

Pull out those scripts one more time. Turn to page 189. Read Daniel 12:8-13 and mark the key words from the box below on your Observation Worksheet. Add any new keywords to your key-word bookmark.

Key Words for Daniel 12:8-13

Daniel (color it blue)

man dressed in linen (box it in blue and color it yellow)

the end time (circle it in green and color it red)

---

those who have insight (color it orange)

regular sacrifice (color it pink)

abomination of desolation (color it red)

Don't forget to mark your pronouns! And mark anything that tells you WHEN by drawing a green clock ⏰ or green circle like this: ⚪ .

Now come in tight on Daniel to capture his expression.

Daniel 12:8 WHAT does Daniel ask?

_____

Daniel 12:9 HOW does the man dressed in linen respond? WHAT do we see about these words?

_____

HOW long are these words sealed up?

_____

Daniel 12:10 WHAT will happen to many?

_____

WHAT will happen to the wicked?

_____

WHO will understand?_____

Daniel 12:11 WHAT will be abolished?

_____

WHAT will be set up?

_____

Uh-oh, we've seen this before! Remember how we saw the prince who is to come in Daniel 9:27 stop the regular sacrifices in the middle of the week? And we saw the Abomination of Desolation standing in the holy place in Matthew 24. The holy place is the holy of holies, the most holy place where the ark of the covenant was. It is a picture of God's throne. Before we wrap this up, do you know the other two names that this prince who is to come, the Abomination of Desolation, is called in the Bible? Let's take a minute to find out. Look up and read 2 Thessalonians 2:3-4,8.

2 Thessalonians 2:3 WHO will be revealed?

_____

WHAT else is he called?

The _____ of _____

2 Thessalonians 2:4 WHAT does this man of lawlessness do?

_____

_____

_____

Unbelievable! This sounds just like the Abomination of Desolation standing in the holy place! Can you imagine someone so bold, so evil, that he would stand in God's temple and declare himself to be God?

Are you blown away? Look at what you have discovered. You know that the little horn in Daniel 7 is the prince who is to come in Daniel 9, the beast in Revelation 13, the Abomination of Desolation in Matthew 24, and the man of lawlessness in 2 Thessalonians 2. Did you also know he is called another name, one that you have probably heard before? He is called the Antichrist in 1 John 2:22. Are you surprised, or did you figure out before now that this person would be the Antichrist?

Look back at Daniel 12:11.

HOW many days will there be from when the regular sacrifice is abolished and the abomination of desolation is set up?

_____

This time period is 30 days longer than our 3½ years. Some people believe that this extra 30 days may have something to do with events surrounding the coming of the Ancient of Days and the setting up of His kingdom, but we don't really know for sure because the Bible doesn't tell us.

Daniel 12:12 WHO is blessed?

_____

We don't know for sure what this blessing is for those who reach the 1335 days. This could be for those who persevere through the judgment of the nations and the separation of the sheep from the goats that is described in Matthew 25.

Daniel 12:13 WHAT will happen to Daniel?

_____

Wow! God shows Daniel he will enter into rest and rise again for his allotted portion. Isn't that incredible? God's going to resurrect Daniel from the dead and reward him!

All the way up to the very end there will be very hard and difficult times for Daniel's people, but those who hang in there, those who have insight, those who believe in Jesus will go into everlasting life. They will receive the everlasting kingdom!

Now ask yourself: HOW am I going to live, now that I know God's plan for the future? Your memory verse, Daniel 12:3, says, *"Those who have insight will shine brightly like the brightness of the expanse of heaven, and those who lead the many to righteousness, like the stars forever and ever."*

Will you be like the ones who have insight in Daniel? Will you shine like the stars? You can shine by studying God's Word, hiding it in your heart, and obeying it. You can be kind to all the kids in your school and not just to your friends, especially to those who are left out or different. You can shine by showing them Jesus by the way you treat them, by talking to them, and by inviting them to hang out with you. You can also shine by the way you treat adults. Do you give your teachers respect? Do you obey your parents? Write out a way you are going to shine for Jesus.

_____

_____

Will you lead others to righteousness? You can lead others to righteousness by doing what God says is right: by teaching kids about Jesus or how to study the Bible like you do, by being a good example, by telling the truth to your parents and teachers, by not cheating, by not talking about kids behind their backs or making fun of them.

Write out a way you will lead others to righteousness.

_____

_____

Now say your memory verse to a grown-up. Are you ready to be a Daniel? Will you display strength and take action?

Cut! Awesome work! We are so proud of you!

it's a wrap!

Way to go! You did it! You helped film an incredible television series that will show people everywhere the amazing events that will take place before Jesus returns to set up His kingdom on earth!

Just look at all you have discovered. You know that God has a perfect plan for the future to bring about His kingdom on earth. He is in control over time and all events!

You also got to fast-forward into the future as God gave King Nebuchadnezzar a dream of a statue that showed four kingdoms that would come. Won't it be awesome when that stone finally crushes those ten toes, the ten kings?

Were you amazed at Daniel's visions and those four ferocious beasts? Just look at how God gave him details of what would happen in the future. God showed Daniel the four Gentile kingdoms and gave him a vision about 70 weeks for his people and the holy city. Sixty-nine of those weeks have already been fulfilled. There is only one more week to go in the 70 weeks. One day soon the "prince who is to come" will come upon the scene, make a covenant with the many, and break it in the middle of the week, while a time of distress that has never been seen before will come upon the whole earth. Wow!

But you also know what is going to happen to him at the end of time. Jesus will crush this "prince who is to come," the little horn's kingdom. His dominion will be taken away, he will be annihilated and destroyed forever, and the kingdom will be given to the saints of the Highest One forever! Hooray!

Just remember that God is in control over all the events that will take place on the earth. You have nothing to fear if you are a believer in Jesus Christ. Your future in heaven is secure in Him!

Don't forget to fill out the card in the back of this book. We have something special that we want to send you for hanging in there through visions of a statue, a lion, a bear, a leopard, a D.T. beast, all kinds of horns, a ram, a goat, kings, and a prince who is to come so you could understand God's plan for the future. We are so very proud of you! Keep up the good work. Dare to be a Daniel in your world! See you for another adventure in God's Word real soon!

Molly, Max, and

(Sam)

P.S. Now, that you have finished Daniel, you may want to solve the mystery of Revelation in *Bible Prophecy for Kids!* and *A Sneak Peek into the Future*.

Four beasts for page 39.

Ram and goat for page 61.

Page 14

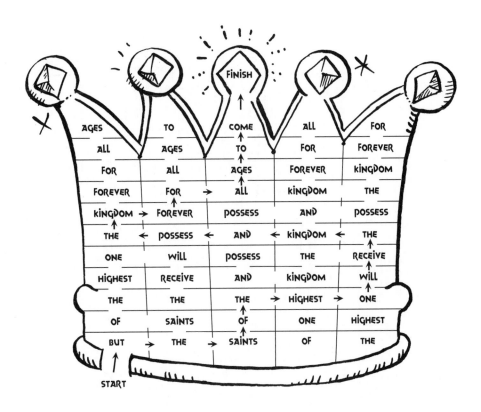

"But the saints of the Highest One will receive the kingdom and possess the kingdom forever, for all ages to come."

Daniel 7:18

Page 18
See page 166.

Page 36

"But the *court* will sit for *judgment,* and *his dominion* will be *taken away, annihilated* and *destroyed forever."*

Daniel 7:26

Page 50

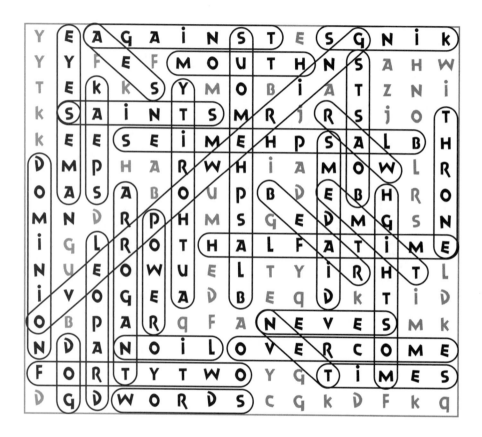

Page 65

"The ram which you saw with the two horns represents the kings of Media and Persia. The shaggy goat represents the kingdom of Greece, and the large horn that is between his eyes is the first king."

Daniel 8:20-21

Page 76

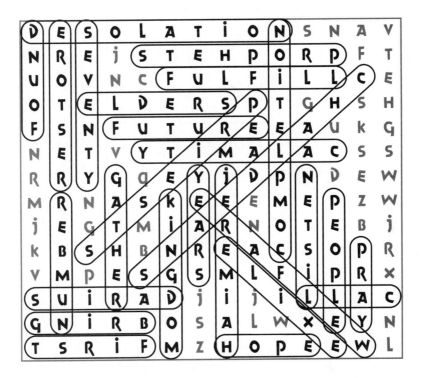

Page 77

"As it is written in the law of Moses, all this calamity has come on us; yet we have not sought the favor of the LORD our God by turning from our iniquity and giving attention to Your truth."

Daniel 9:13

Page 79

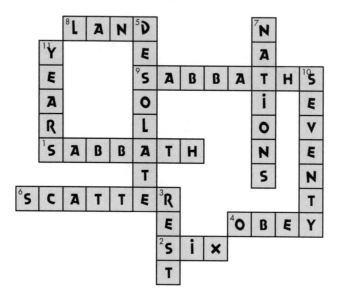

Page 97

"Now I have come to give you an understanding of what will happen to your people in the latter days, for the vision pertains to the days yet future."

Daniel 10:14

Page 107
See page 167.

Page 117

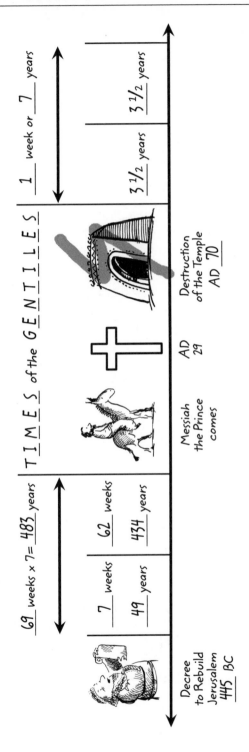

TiME GAP

T I M E S of the G E N T I L E S

Decree
to Rebuild
Jerusalem
445 BC

7 weeks
49 years

62 weeks
434 years

69 weeks × 7 = 483 years

Messiah
the Prince
comes

AD
29

Destruction
of the Temple
AD 70

1 week or 7 years

3 ½ years

3 ½ years

Completed Chart from page 18

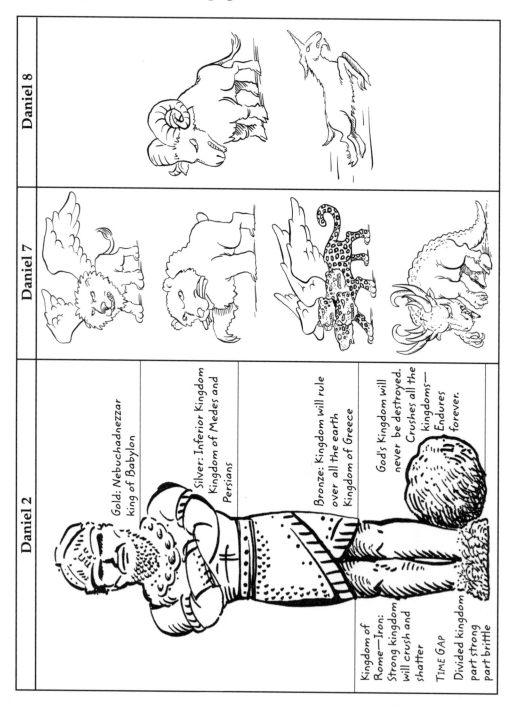

Daniel 2	Daniel 7	Daniel 8

Daniel 2

Gold: Nebuchadnezzar king of Babylon

Silver: Inferior Kingdom Kingdom of Medes and Persians

Bronze: Kingdom will rule over all the earth Kingdom of Greece

God's Kingdom will never be destroyed. Crushes all the kingdoms— Endures forever.

Kingdom of Rome—Iron: Strong kingdom will crush and shatter

TIME GAP

Divided kingdom part strong part brittle

Page 125

"But the people who know their God will display strength and take action."

Daniel 11:32b

Page 140

"Those who have insight will shine brightly like the brightness of the expanse of heaven, and those who lead the many to righteousness, like the stars forever and ever."

Daniel 12:3

Page 107

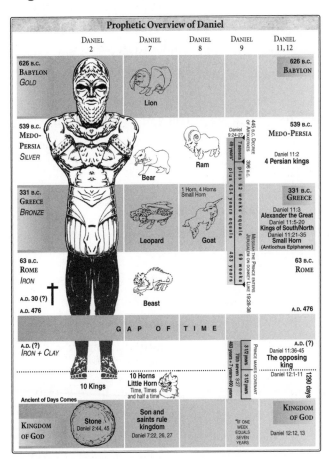

OBSERVATION WORKSHEETS
DANIEL 2,7-12

Chapter 2

1 Now in the second year of the reign of Nebuchadnezzar, Nebuchadnezzar had dreams; and his spirit was troubled and his sleep left him.

2 Then the king gave orders to call in the magicians, the conjurers, the sorcerers and the Chaldeans to tell the king his dreams. So they came in and stood before the king.

3 The king said to them, "I had a dream and my spirit is anxious to understand the dream."

4 Then the Chaldeans spoke to the king in Aramaic: "O king, live forever! Tell the dream to your servants, and we will declare the interpretation."

5 The king replied to the Chaldeans, "The command from me is firm: if you do not make known to me the dream and its interpretation, you will be torn limb from limb and your houses will be made a rubbish heap.

6 "But if you declare the dream and its interpretation, you will receive from me gifts and a reward and great honor; therefore declare to me the dream and its interpretation."

7 They answered a second time and said, "Let the king tell the dream to his servants, and we will declare the interpretation."

8 The king replied, "I know for certain that you are bargaining for time, inasmuch as you have seen that the command from me is firm,

9 that if you do not make the dream known to me, there is only one decree for you. For you have agreed together to speak lying and corrupt words before me until the situation is changed; there-

fore tell me the dream, that I may know that you can declare to me its interpretation."

10 The Chaldeans answered the king and said, "There is not a man on earth who could declare the matter for the king, inasmuch as no great king or ruler has ever asked anything like this of any magician, conjurer or Chaldean.

11 "Moreover, the thing which the king demands is difficult, and there is no one else who could declare it to the king except gods, whose dwelling place is not with mortal flesh."

12 Because of this the king became indignant and very furious and gave orders to destroy all the wise men of Babylon.

13 So the decree went forth that the wise men should be slain; and they looked for Daniel and his friends to kill them.

14 Then Daniel replied with discretion and discernment to Arioch, the captain of the king's bodyguard, who had gone forth to slay the wise men of Babylon;

15 he said to Arioch, the king's commander, "For what reason is the decree from the king so urgent?" Then Arioch informed Daniel about the matter.

16 So Daniel went in and requested of the king that he would give him time, in order that he might declare the interpretation to the king.

17 Then Daniel went to his house and informed his friends, Hananiah, Mishael and Azariah, about the matter,

18 so that they might request compassion from the God of heaven concerning this mystery, so that Daniel and his friends would not be destroyed with the rest of the wise men of Babylon.

19 Then the mystery was revealed to Daniel in a night vision. Then Daniel blessed the God of heaven;

20 Daniel said, "Let the name of God be blessed forever and ever, For wisdom and power belong to Him.

21 "It is He who changes the times and the epochs; He removes kings and establishes kings; He gives wisdom to wise men And knowledge to men of understanding.

22 "It is He who reveals the profound and hidden things; He knows what is in the darkness, And the light dwells with Him.

23 "To You, O God of my fathers, I give thanks and praise, For You have given me wisdom and power; Even now You have made known to me what we requested of You, For You have made known to us the king's matter."

24 Therefore, Daniel went in to Arioch, whom the king had appointed to destroy the wise men of Babylon; he went and spoke to him as follows: "Do not destroy the wise men of Babylon! Take me into the king's presence, and I will declare the interpretation to the king."

25 Then Arioch hurriedly brought Daniel into the king's presence and spoke to him as follows: "I have found a man among the exiles from Judah who can make the interpretation known to the king!"

26 The king said to Daniel, whose name was Belteshazzar, "Are you able to make known to me the dream which I have seen and its interpretation?"

27 Daniel answered before the king and said, "As for the mystery about which the king has inquired, neither wise men, conjurers, magicians nor diviners are able to declare it to the king.

28 "However, there is a God in heaven who reveals mysteries, and He has made known to King Nebuchadnezzar what will take place in the latter days. This was your dream and the visions in your mind while on your bed.

29 "As for you, O king, while on your bed your thoughts turned to what would take place in the future; and He who reveals mysteries has made known to you what will take place.

30 "But as for me, this mystery has not been revealed to me for any

wisdom residing in me more than in any other living man, but for the purpose of making the interpretation known to the king, and that you may understand the thoughts of your mind.

31 "You, O king, were looking and behold, there was a single great statue; that statue, which was large and of extraordinary splendor, was standing in front of you, and its appearance was awesome.

32 "The head of that statue was made of fine gold, its breast and its arms of silver, its belly and its thighs of bronze,

33 its legs of iron, its feet partly of iron and partly of clay.

34 "You continued looking until a stone was cut out without hands, and it struck the statue on its feet of iron and clay and crushed them.

35 "Then the iron, the clay, the bronze, the silver and the gold were crushed all at the same time and became like chaff from the summer threshing floors; and the wind carried them away so that not a trace of them was found. But the stone that struck the statue became a great mountain and filled the whole earth.

36 "This was the dream; now we will tell its interpretation before the king.

37 "You, O king, are the king of kings, to whom the God of heaven has given the kingdom, the power, the strength and the glory;

38 and wherever the sons of men dwell, or the beasts of the field, or the birds of the sky, He has given them into your hand and has caused you to rule over them all. You are the head of gold.

39 "After you there will arise another kingdom inferior to you, then another third kingdom of bronze, which will rule over all the earth.

40 "Then there will be a fourth kingdom as strong as iron; inasmuch as iron crushes and shatters all things, so, like iron that breaks in pieces, it will crush and break all these in pieces.

41 "In that you saw the feet and toes, partly of potter's clay and partly of iron, it will be a divided kingdom; but it will have in it

the toughness of iron, inasmuch as you saw the iron mixed with common clay.

42 "As the toes of the feet were partly of iron and partly of pottery, so some of the kingdom will be strong and part of it will be brittle.

43 "And in that you saw the iron mixed with common clay, they will combine with one another in the seed of men; but they will not adhere to one another, even as iron does not combine with pottery.

44 "In the days of those kings the God of heaven will set up a kingdom which will never be destroyed, and that kingdom will not be left for another people; it will crush and put an end to all these kingdoms, but it will itself endure forever.

45 "Inasmuch as you saw that a stone was cut out of the mountain without hands and that it crushed the iron, the bronze, the clay, the silver and the gold, the great God has made known to the king what will take place in the future; so the dream is true and its interpretation is trustworthy."

46 Then King Nebuchadnezzar fell on his face and did homage to Daniel, and gave orders to present to him an offering and fragrant incense.

47 The king answered Daniel and said, "Surely your God is a God of gods and a Lord of kings and a revealer of mysteries, since you have been able to reveal this mystery."

48 Then the king promoted Daniel and gave him many great gifts, and he made him ruler over the whole province of Babylon and chief prefect over all the wise men of Babylon.

49 And Daniel made request of the king, and he appointed Shadrach, Meshach and Abed-nego over the administration of the province of Babylon, while Daniel was at the king's court.

Chapter 7

1 In the first year of Belshazzar king of Babylon Daniel saw a

dream and visions in his mind as he lay on his bed; then he wrote the dream down and related the following summary of it.

2 Daniel said, "I was looking in my vision by night, and behold, the four winds of heaven were stirring up the great sea.

3 "And four great beasts were coming up from the sea, different from one another.

4 "The first was like a lion and had the wings of an eagle. I kept looking until its wings were plucked, and it was lifted up from the ground and made to stand on two feet like a man; a human mind also was given to it.

5 "And behold, another beast, a second one, resembling a bear. And it was raised up on one side, and three ribs were in its mouth between its teeth; and thus they said to it, 'Arise, devour much meat!'

6 "After this I kept looking, and behold, another one, like a leopard, which had on its back four wings of a bird; the beast also had four heads, and dominion was given to it.

7 "After this I kept looking in the night visions, and behold, a fourth beast, dreadful and terrifying and extremely strong; and it had large iron teeth. It devoured and crushed and trampled down the remainder with its feet; and it was different from all the beasts that were before it, and it had ten horns.

8 "While I was contemplating the horns, behold, another horn, a little one, came up among them, and three of the first horns were pulled out by the roots before it; and behold, this horn possessed eyes like the eyes of a man and a mouth uttering great boasts.

9 "I kept looking Until thrones were set up, And the Ancient of Days took His seat; His vesture was like white snow And the hair of His head like pure wool. His throne was ablaze with flames, Its wheels were a burning fire.

10 "A river of fire was flowing And coming out from before Him;

Thousands upon thousands were attending Him, And myriads
upon myriads were standing before Him; The court sat,
And the books were opened.

11 "Then I kept looking because of the sound of the boastful words
which the horn was speaking; I kept looking until the beast was slain,
and its body was destroyed and given to the burning fire.

12 "As for the rest of the beasts, their dominion was taken away,
but an extension of life was granted to them for an appointed
period of time.

13 "I kept looking in the night visions, And behold, with the
clouds of heaven One like a Son of Man was coming, And He came
up to the Ancient of Days And was presented before Him.

14 "And to Him was given dominion, Glory and a kingdom, That
all the peoples, nations and men of every language Might serve
Him. His dominion is an everlasting dominion Which will not pass
away; And His kingdom is one Which will not be destroyed.

15 "As for me, Daniel, my spirit was distressed within me, and the
visions in my mind kept alarming me.

16 "I approached one of those who were standing by and began
asking him the exact meaning of all this. So he told me and made
known to me the interpretation of these things:

17 'These great beasts, which are four in number, are four kings
who will arise from the earth.

18 'But the saints of the Highest One will receive the kingdom and
possess the kingdom forever, for all ages to come.'

19 "Then I desired to know the exact meaning of the fourth beast,
which was different from all the others, exceedingly dreadful,
with its teeth of iron and its claws of bronze, and which devoured,
crushed and trampled down the remainder with its feet,

20 and the meaning of the ten horns that were on its head and
the other horn which came up, and before which three of them

fell, namely, that horn which had eyes and a mouth uttering great boasts and which was larger in appearance than its associates.

21 "I kept looking, and that horn was waging war with the saints and overpowering them

22 until the Ancient of Days came and judgment was passed in favor of the saints of the Highest One, and the time arrived when the saints took possession of the kingdom.

23 "Thus he said: 'The fourth beast will be a fourth kingdom on the earth, which will be different from all the other kingdoms and will devour the whole earth and tread it down and crush it.

24 'As for the ten horns, out of this kingdom ten kings will arise; and another will arise after them, and he will be different from the previous ones and will subdue three kings.

25 'He will speak out against the Most High and wear down the saints of the Highest One, and he will intend to make alterations in times and in law; and they will be given into his hand for a time, times, and half a time.

26 'But the court will sit for judgment, and his dominion will be taken away, annihilated and destroyed forever.

27 'Then the sovereignty, the dominion and the greatness of all the kingdoms under the whole heaven will be given to the people of the saints of the Highest One; His kingdom will be an everlasting kingdom, and all the dominions will serve and obey Him.'

28 "At this point the revelation ended. As for me, Daniel, my thoughts were greatly alarming me and my face grew pale, but I kept the matter to myself."

Chapter 8

1 In the third year of the reign of Belshazzar the king a vision appeared to me, Daniel, subsequent to the one which appeared to me previously.

2 I looked in the vision, and while I was looking I was in the citadel of Susa, which is in the province of Elam; and I looked in the vision and I myself was beside the Ulai Canal.

3 Then I lifted my eyes and looked, and behold, a ram which had two horns was standing in front of the canal. Now the two horns were long, but one was longer than the other, with the longer one coming up last.

4 I saw the ram butting westward, northward, and southward, and no other beasts could stand before him nor was there anyone to rescue from his power, but he did as he pleased and magnified himself.

5 While I was observing, behold, a male goat was coming from the west over the surface of the whole earth without touching the ground; and the goat had a conspicuous horn between his eyes.

6 He came up to the ram that had the two horns, which I had seen standing in front of the canal, and rushed at him in his mighty wrath.

7 I saw him come beside the ram, and he was enraged at him; and he struck the ram and shattered his two horns, and the ram had no strength to withstand him. So he hurled him to the ground and trampled on him, and there was none to rescue the ram from his power.

8 Then the male goat magnified himself exceedingly. But as soon as he was mighty, the large horn was broken; and in its place there came up four conspicuous horns toward the four winds of heaven.

9 Out of one of them came forth a rather small horn which grew exceedingly great toward the south, toward the east, and toward the Beautiful Land.

10 It grew up to the host of heaven and caused some of the host and some of the stars to fall to the earth, and it trampled them down.

11 It even magnified itself to be equal with the Commander of the host; and it removed the regular sacrifice from Him, and the place of His sanctuary was thrown down.

12 And on account of transgression the host will be given over to the horn along with the regular sacrifice; and it will fling truth to the ground and perform its will and prosper.

13 Then I heard a holy one speaking, and another holy one said to that particular one who was speaking, "How long will the vision about the regular sacrifice apply, while the transgression causes horror, so as to allow both the holy place and the host to be trampled?"

14 He said to me, "For 2,300 evenings and mornings; then the holy place will be properly restored."

15 When I, Daniel, had seen the vision, I sought to understand it; and behold, standing before me was one who looked like a man.

16 And I heard the voice of a man between the banks of Ulai, and he called out and said, "Gabriel, give this man an understanding of the vision."

17 So he came near to where I was standing, and when he came I was frightened and fell on my face; but he said to me, "Son of man, understand that the vision pertains to the time of the end."

18 Now while he was talking with me, I sank into a deep sleep with my face to the ground; but he touched me and made me stand upright.

19 He said, "Behold, I am going to let you know what will occur at the final period of the indignation, for it pertains to the appointed time of the end.

20 "The ram which you saw with the two horns represents the kings of Media and Persia.

21 "The shaggy goat represents the kingdom of Greece, and the large horn that is between his eyes is the first king.

22 "The broken horn and the four horns that arose in its place represent four kingdoms which will arise from his nation, although not with his power.

23 "In the latter period of their rule, When the transgressors have run their course, A king will arise, Insolent and skilled in intrigue.

24 "His power will be mighty, but not by his own power, And he will destroy to an extraordinary degree And prosper and perform his will; He will destroy mighty men and the holy people.

25 "And through his shrewdness He will cause deceit to succeed by his influence; And he will magnify himself in his heart, And he will destroy many while they are at ease. He will even oppose the Prince of princes, But he will be broken without human agency.

26 "The vision of the evenings and mornings Which has been told is true; But keep the vision secret, For it pertains to many days in the future."

27 Then I, Daniel, was exhausted and sick for days. Then I got up again and carried on the king's business; but I was astounded at the vision, and there was none to explain it.

Chapter 9

1 In the first year of Darius the son of Ahasuerus, of Median descent, who was made king over the kingdom of the Chaldeans—

2 in the first year of his reign, I, Daniel, observed in the books the number of the years which was revealed as the word of the LORD to Jeremiah the prophet for the completion of the desolations of Jerusalem, namely, seventy years.

3 So I gave my attention to the Lord God to seek Him by prayer and supplications, with fasting, sackcloth and ashes.

4 I prayed to the LORD my God and confessed and said, "Alas, O Lord, the great and awesome God, who keeps His covenant and

lovingkindness for those who love Him and keep His commandments,

5 we have sinned, committed iniquity, acted wickedly and rebelled, even turning aside from Your commandments and ordinances.

6 "Moreover, we have not listened to Your servants the prophets, who spoke in Your name to our kings, our princes, our fathers and all the people of the land.

7 "Righteousness belongs to You, O Lord, but to us open shame, as it is this day—to the men of Judah, the inhabitants of Jerusalem and all Israel, those who are nearby and those who are far away in all the countries to which You have driven them, because of their unfaithful deeds which they have committed against You.

8 "Open shame belongs to us, O Lord, to our kings, our princes and our fathers, because we have sinned against You.

9 "To the Lord our God belong compassion and forgiveness, for we have rebelled against Him;

10 nor have we obeyed the voice of the LORD our God, to walk in His teachings which He set before us through His servants the prophets.

11 "Indeed all Israel has transgressed Your law and turned aside, not obeying Your voice; so the curse has been poured out on us, along with the oath which is written in the law of Moses the servant of God, for we have sinned against Him.

12 "Thus He has confirmed His words which He had spoken against us and against our rulers who ruled us, to bring on us great calamity; for under the whole heaven there has not been done anything like what was done to Jerusalem.

13 "As it is written in the law of Moses, all this calamity has come on us; yet we have not sought the favor of the LORD our God by turning from our iniquity and giving attention to Your truth.

14 "Therefore the LORD has kept the calamity in store and brought it on us; for the LORD our God is righteous with respect to all His deeds which He has done, but we have not obeyed His voice.

15 "And now, O Lord our God, who have brought Your people out of the land of Egypt with a mighty hand and have made a name for Yourself, as it is this day—we have sinned, we have been wicked.

16 "O Lord, in accordance with all Your righteous acts, let now Your anger and Your wrath turn away from Your city Jerusalem, Your holy mountain; for because of our sins and the iniquities of our fathers, Jerusalem and Your people have become a reproach to all those around us.

17 "So now, our God, listen to the prayer of Your servant and to his supplications, and for Your sake, O Lord, let Your face shine on Your desolate sanctuary.

18 "O my God, incline Your ear and hear! Open Your eyes and see our desolations and the city which is called by Your name; for we are not presenting our supplications before You on account of any merits of our own, but on account of Your great compassion.

19 "O Lord, hear! O Lord, forgive! O Lord, listen and take action! For Your own sake, O my God, do not delay, because Your city and Your people are called by Your name."

20 Now while I was speaking and praying, and confessing my sin and the sin of my people Israel, and presenting my supplication before the LORD my God in behalf of the holy mountain of my God,

21 while I was still speaking in prayer, then the man Gabriel, whom I had seen in the vision previously, came to me in my extreme weariness about the time of the evening offering.

22 He gave me instruction and talked with me and said, "O Daniel, I have now come forth to give you insight with understanding.

23 "At the beginning of your supplications the command was

issued, and I have come to tell you, for you are highly esteemed; so give heed to the message and gain understanding of the vision.

24 "Seventy weeks have been decreed for your people and your holy city, to finish the transgression, to make an end of sin, to make atonement for iniquity, to bring in everlasting righteousness, to seal up vision and prophecy and to anoint the most holy place.

25 "So you are to know and discern that from the issuing of a decree to restore and rebuild Jerusalem until Messiah the Prince there will be seven weeks and sixty-two weeks; it will be built again, with plaza and moat, even in times of distress.

26 "Then after the sixty-two weeks the Messiah will be cut off and have nothing, and the people of the prince who is to come will destroy the city and the sanctuary. And its end will come with a flood; even to the end there will be war; desolations are determined.

27 "And he will make a firm covenant with the many for one week, but in the middle of the week he will put a stop to sacrifice and grain offering; and on the wing of abominations will come one who makes desolate, even until a complete destruction, one that is decreed, is poured out on the one who makes desolate."

Chapter 10

1 In the third year of Cyrus king of Persia a message was revealed to Daniel, who was named Belteshazzar; and the message was true and one of great conflict, but he understood the message and had an understanding of the vision.

2 In those days, I, Daniel, had been mourning for three entire weeks.

3 I did not eat any tasty food, nor did meat or wine enter my mouth, nor did I use any ointment at all until the entire three weeks were completed.

4 On the twenty-fourth day of the first month, while I was by the bank of the great river, that is, the Tigris,

5 I lifted my eyes and looked, and behold, there was a certain man dressed in linen, whose waist was girded with a belt of pure gold of Uphaz.

6 His body also was like beryl, his face had the appearance of lightning, his eyes were like flaming torches, his arms and feet like the gleam of polished bronze, and the sound of his words like the sound of a tumult.

7 Now I, Daniel, alone saw the vision, while the men who were with me did not see the vision; nevertheless, a great dread fell on them, and they ran away to hide themselves.

8 So I was left alone and saw this great vision; yet no strength was left in me, for my natural color turned to a deathly pallor, and I retained no strength.

9 But I heard the sound of his words; and as soon as I heard the sound of his words, I fell into a deep sleep on my face, with my face to the ground.

10 Then behold, a hand touched me and set me trembling on my hands and knees.

11 He said to me, "O Daniel, man of high esteem, understand the words that I am about to tell you and stand upright, for I have now been sent to you." And when he had spoken this word to me, I stood up trembling.

12 Then he said to me, "Do not be afraid, Daniel, for from the first day that you set your heart on understanding this and on humbling yourself before your God, your words were heard, and I have come in response to your words.

13 "But the prince of the kingdom of Persia was withstanding me for twenty-one days; then behold, Michael, one of the chief princes, came to help me, for I had been left there with the kings of Persia.

14 "Now I have come to give you an understanding of what will happen to your people in the latter days, for the vision pertains to the days yet future."

15 When he had spoken to me according to these words, I turned my face toward the ground and became speechless.

16 And behold, one who resembled a human being was touching my lips; then I opened my mouth and spoke and said to him who was standing before me, "O my lord, as a result of the vision anguish has come upon me, and I have retained no strength.

17 "For how can such a servant of my lord talk with such as my lord? As for me, there remains just now no strength in me, nor has any breath been left in me."

18 Then this one with human appearance touched me again and strengthened me.

19 He said, "O man of high esteem, do not be afraid. Peace be with you; take courage and be courageous!" Now as soon as he spoke to me, I received strength and said, "May my lord speak, for you have strengthened me."

20 Then he said, "Do you understand why I came to you? But I shall now return to fight against the prince of Persia; so I am going forth, and behold, the prince of Greece is about to come.

21 "However, I will tell you what is inscribed in the writing of truth. Yet there is no one who stands firmly with me against these forces except Michael your prince.

Chapter 11

1 "In the first year of Darius the Mede, I arose to be an encouragement and a protection for him.

2 "And now I will tell you the truth. Behold, three more kings are going to arise in Persia. Then a fourth will gain far more riches than

all of them; as soon as he becomes strong through his riches, he will arouse the whole empire against the realm of Greece.

3 "And a mighty king will arise, and he will rule with great authority and do as he pleases.

4 "But as soon as he has arisen, his kingdom will be broken up and parceled out toward the four points of the compass, though not to his own descendants, nor according to his authority which he wielded, for his sovereignty will be uprooted and given to others besides them.

5 "Then the king of the South will grow strong, along with one of his princes who will gain ascendancy over him and obtain dominion; his domain will be a great dominion indeed.

6 "After some years they will form an alliance, and the daughter of the king of the South will come to the king of the North to carry out a peaceful arrangement. But she will not retain her position of power, nor will he remain with his power, but she will be given up, along with those who brought her in and the one who sired her as well as he who supported her in those times.

7 "But one of the descendants of her line will arise in his place, and he will come against their army and enter the fortress of the king of the North, and he will deal with them and display great strength.

8 "Also their gods with their metal images and their precious vessels of silver and gold he will take into captivity to Egypt, and he on his part will refrain from attacking the king of the North for some years.

9 "Then the latter will enter the realm of the king of the South, but will return to his own land.

10 "His sons will mobilize and assemble a multitude of great forces; and one of them will keep on coming and overflow and pass through, that he may again wage war up to his very fortress.

11 "The king of the South will be enraged and go forth and fight

with the king of the North. Then the latter will raise a great multitude, but that multitude will be given into the hand of the former.
12 "When the multitude is carried away, his heart will be lifted up, and he will cause tens of thousands to fall; yet he will not prevail.
13 "For the king of the North will again raise a greater multitude than the former, and after an interval of some years he will press on with a great army and much equipment.
14 "Now in those times many will rise up against the king of the South; the violent ones among your people will also lift themselves up in order to fulfill the vision, but they will fall down.
15 "Then the king of the North will come, cast up a siege ramp and capture a well-fortified city; and the forces of the South will not stand their ground, not even their choicest troops, for there will be no strength to make a stand.
16 "But he who comes against him will do as he pleases, and no one will be able to withstand him; he will also stay for a time in the Beautiful Land, with destruction in his hand.
17 "He will set his face to come with the power of his whole kingdom, bringing with him a proposal of peace which he will put into effect; he will also give him the daughter of women to ruin it. But she will not take a stand for him or be on his side.
18 "Then he will turn his face to the coastlands and capture many. But a commander will put a stop to his scorn against him; moreover, he will repay him for his scorn.
19 "So he will turn his face toward the fortresses of his own land, but he will stumble and fall and be found no more.
20 "Then in his place one will arise who will send an oppressor through the Jewel of his kingdom; yet within a few days he will be shattered, though not in anger nor in battle.
21 "In his place a despicable person will arise, on whom the honor

of kingship has not been conferred, but he will come in a time of tranquility and seize the kingdom by intrigue.

22 "The overflowing forces will be flooded away before him and shattered, and also the prince of the covenant.

23 "After an alliance is made with him he will practice deception, and he will go up and gain power with a small force of people.

24 "In a time of tranquility he will enter the richest parts of the realm, and he will accomplish what his fathers never did, nor his ancestors; he will distribute plunder, booty and possessions among them, and he will devise his schemes against strongholds, but only for a time.

25 "He will stir up his strength and courage against the king of the South with a large army; so the king of the South will mobilize an extremely large and mighty army for war; but he will not stand, for schemes will be devised against him.

26 "Those who eat his choice food will destroy him, and his army will overflow, but many will fall down slain.

27 "As for both kings, their hearts will be intent on evil, and they will speak lies to each other at the same table; but it will not succeed, for the end is still to come at the appointed time.

28 "Then he will return to his land with much plunder; but his heart will be set against the holy covenant, and he will take action and then return to his own land.

29 "At the appointed time he will return and come into the South, but this last time it will not turn out the way it did before.

30 "For ships of Kittim will come against him; therefore he will be disheartened and will return and become enraged at the holy covenant and take action; so he will come back and show regard for those who forsake the holy covenant.

31 "Forces from him will arise, desecrate the sanctuary fortress, and

do away with the regular sacrifice. And they will set up the abomination of desolation.

32 "By smooth words he will turn to godlessness those who act wickedly toward the covenant, but the people who know their God will display strength and take action.

33 "Those who have insight among the people will give understanding to the many; yet they will fall by sword and by flame, by captivity and by plunder for many days.

34 "Now when they fall they will be granted a little help, and many will join with them in hypocrisy.

35 "Some of those who have insight will fall, in order to refine, purge and make them pure until the end time; because it is still to come at the appointed time.

36 "Then the king will do as he pleases, and he will exalt and magnify himself above every god and will speak monstrous things against the God of gods; and he will prosper until the indignation is finished, for that which is decreed will be done.

37 "He will show no regard for the gods of his fathers or for the desire of women, nor will he show regard for any other god; for he will magnify himself above them all.

38 "But instead he will honor a god of fortresses, a god whom his fathers did not know; he will honor him with gold, silver, costly stones and treasures.

39 "He will take action against the strongest of fortresses with the help of a foreign god; he will give great honor to those who acknowledge him and will cause them to rule over the many, and will parcel out land for a price.

40 "At the end time the king of the South will collide with him, and the king of the North will storm against him with chariots, with horsemen and with many ships; and he will enter countries, overflow them and pass through.

41 "He will also enter the Beautiful Land, and many countries will fall; but these will be rescued out of his hand: Edom, Moab and the foremost of the sons of Ammon.

42 "Then he will stretch out his hand against other countries, and the land of Egypt will not escape.

43 "But he will gain control over the hidden treasures of gold and silver and over all the precious things of Egypt; and Libyans and Ethiopians will follow at his heels.

44 "But rumors from the East and from the North will disturb him, and he will go forth with great wrath to destroy and annihilate many.

45 "He will pitch the tents of his royal pavilion between the seas and the beautiful Holy Mountain; yet he will come to his end, and no one will help him.

Chapter 12

1 "Now at that time Michael, the great prince who stands guard over the sons of your people, will arise. And there will be a time of distress such as never occurred since there was a nation until that time; and at that time your people, everyone who is found written in the book, will be rescued.

2 "Many of those who sleep in the dust of the ground will awake, these to everlasting life, but the others to disgrace and everlasting contempt.

3 "Those who have insight will shine brightly like the brightness of the expanse of heaven, and those who lead the many to righteousness, like the stars forever and ever.

4 "But as for you, Daniel, conceal these words and seal up the book until the end of time; many will go back and forth, and knowledge will increase."

5 Then I, Daniel, looked and behold, two others were standing, one on this bank of the river and the other on that bank of the river.

6 And one said to the man dressed in linen, who was above the waters of the river, "How long will it be until the end of these wonders?"

7 I heard the man dressed in linen, who was above the waters of the river, as he raised his right hand and his left toward heaven, and swore by Him who lives forever that it would be for a time, times, and half a time; and as soon as they finish shattering the power of the holy people, all these events will be completed.

8 As for me, I heard but could not understand; so I said, "My lord, what will be the outcome of these events?"

9 He said, "Go your way, Daniel, for these words are concealed and sealed up until the end time.

10 "Many will be purged, purified and refined, but the wicked will act wickedly; and none of the wicked will understand, but those who have insight will understand.

11 "From the time that the regular sacrifice is abolished and the abomination of desolation is set up, there will be 1,290 days.

12 "How blessed is he who keeps waiting and attains to the 1,335 days!

13 "But as for you, go your way to the end; then you will enter into rest and rise again for your allotted portion at the end of the age."

DISCOVER 4 YOURSELF!®
INDUCTIVE BIBLE STUDIES FOR KIDS

Bible study can be fun! Now kids can learn how to inductively study the Bible to discover for themselves what it says. Each book combines serious Bible study with memorable games, puzzles, and activities that reinforce biblical truth. Divided into short lessons, each individual study includes:

- a weekly memory verse
- Bible knowledge activities—puzzles, games, and discovery activities
- optional crafts and projects to help kids practice what they've learned

Any young person who works through these studies will emerge with a richer appreciation for the Word of God and a deeper understanding of God's love and care.

Perfect for Sunday school classes, children's Bible studies, homeschooling, and individual study.

Kay Arthur and Janna Arndt
Kids create a TV show based on Daniel 1–6. They do fun activities while learning about dreams and beasts and the future.
ISBN 978-0-7369-0147-5

Kay Arthur and Janna Arndt
Kids continue the TV show based on Daniel 7–12. They draw storyboards and do other fun puzzles while learning about Daniel's prophecies.
ISBN 978-0-7369-2285-2

Kay Arthur and Cyndy Shearer
Kids "make" a movie to discover who Jesus is and His impact on their lives. Activities and 15-minute lessons make this study of John 1–10 great for all ages!
ISBN 978-0-7369-0119-2

Kay Arthur and Scoti Domeij
As "reporters," kids investigate Jonah's story and conduct interviews. Using puzzles and activities, these lessons highlight God's loving care and the importance of obedience.
ISBN 978-0-7369-0203-8

Kay Arthur and Janna Arndt
Using examples from Joseph's life, games, puzzles, and inductive activities, kids see how God chooses and equips ordinary people to become His superheroes.
ISBN 978-0-7369-0739-2

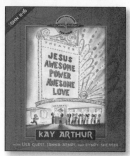

Kay Arthur, Janna Arndt,
Lisa Guest, and Cyndy Shearer

This book picks up where *Jesus in the Spotlight* leaves off: John 11–16. Kids join a movie team to bring the life of Jesus to the big screen in order to learn key truths about prayer, heaven, and Jesus.

ISBN 978-0-7369-0144-4

Kay Arthur and Janna Arndt

As "advice columnists," kids delve into the book of James to discover—and learn how to apply—the best answers for a variety of problems.

ISBN 978-0-7369-0148-2

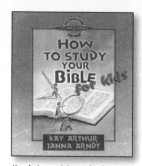

Kay Arthur and Janna Arndt

This easy-to-use Bible study combines serious commitment to God's Word with illustrations and activities that reinforce biblical truth.

ISBN 978-0-7369-0362-2

Kay Arthur and Janna Arndt

Focusing on John 17–21, children become "directors" who must discover the details of Jesus' life to make a great movie. They also learn how to get the most out of reading their Bibles.

ISBN 978-0-7369-0546-6

Kay Arthur and Janna Arndt

Kids become archaeologists to uncover how God deals with sin, where different languages and nations came from, and what God's plan is for saving people (Genesis 3–11).

ISBN 978-0-7369-0374-5

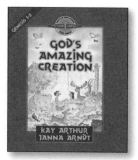

Kay Arthur and Janna Arndt

God's Amazing Creation covers Genesis 1–2—those awesome days when God created the stars, the world, the sea, the animals, and the very first people. Young explorers will go on an archaeological dig to discover truths for themselves!

ISBN 978-0-7369-0143-7

Kay Arthur and Janna Arndt

The Lord's Prayer is the foundation of this special basic training, and it's not long before the trainees discover the awesome truth that God wants to talk to them as much as they want to talk to Him!

ISBN 978-0-7369-0666-1

Kay Arthur and Janna Arndt

Readers head out on the rugged Oregon Trail to discover the lessons Abraham learned when he left his home and moved to an unknown land. Kids will face the excitement, fears, and blessings of faith.

ISBN 978-0-7369-0936-5

Kay Arthur and Janna Arndt

Kids journey to God's heart using the inductive study method and the wonder of an adventurous spy tale.

ISBN 978-0-7369-1161-0

Kay Arthur and Janna Arndt

This engaging, high-energy study examines the journeys of Isaac, Jacob, and Esau and reveals how God outfits His children with everything they need for life's difficulties, victories, and extreme adventures.

ISBN 978-0-7369-0937-2

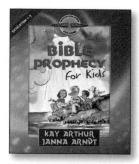

Kay Arthur and Janna Arndt

Kids explore the Bible Discovery Museum and solve the great mysteries about the future using the inductive study method and Revelation 1–7.

ISBN 978-0-7369-1527-4

Kay Arthur and Janna Arndt

Kids tackle Revelation 8–22 in this active and fun Bible study that explores what's to come and the importance of knowing Jesus.

ISBN 978-0-7369-2036-0